The Black River:
Death Poems

The Black River: Death Poems
Edited by Deirdre Pulgram-Arthen

Published by NatureCulture LLC
www.nature-culture.net www.writingtheland.org
ISBN: 978-1-960293-11-4
Hardcover edition
(There is also a paperback edition: 978-1-960293-09-1)
Cover and Interior Artwork: Martin Bridge
Cover design: Lis McLoughlin and Christopher Gendron
Interior design: Lis McLoughlin

Other Publications from NatureCulture

2024
Writing the Land: The Connecticut River
Writing the Land: Wanderings I
Writing the Land: Wanderings II
Writing the Land: Virginia
Writing the Land: Maine II, A Gathering
Cayman Brac From Bluff to Sea

2023
Writing the Land: Youth Write the Land
Writing the Land: Currents
Writing the Land: Channels
Writing the Land: Streamlines
Migrations and Home: The Elements of Place, ed. Simon Wilson
From Root to Seed: Black, Brown, and Indigenous Poets Write the Northeast, ed. Samaa Abdurraqib
The Way of Gaia by Martin Bridge and Steve Trombulak

2022
Writing the Land: Foodways and Social Justice
Writing the Land: Windblown I
Writing the Land: Windblown II
Writing the Land: Maine
LandTrust, poems by Katherine Hagopian Berry

2021, 2024
Writing the Land: Northeast

Forthcoming (2024-2026)
Writing the Land: The Rensselaer Plateau
Writing the Land: Washington
Writing the Land: Doolin, Ireland
Writing the Land: The Cayman Islands
Writing the Land: Horizons

www.nature-culture.net
www.writingtheland.org

The Black River: Death Poems

Edited by Deirdre Pulgram-Arthen

Published by NatureCulture LLC
Northfield, Massachusetts

Speaking of Death
by Susan Barsky Reid

This is the first time I have been asked to write a foreword for a book. But I am under no illusions— this is not about me—it is about the organisation that I represent: I am the media representative and administrator for Death Cafe.

Death Cafe was the brainchild of my late son Jon Underwood who was inspired by the Swiss sociologist Bernard Crettaz. It is a group-directed discussion about death and dying. Any topics within this remit can be discussed, without leading the participants to any conclusion, product or course of action. It is important that this discussion is alongside a cup of tea and delicious cake, a reminder that we are alive and life can be good.

I have hosted many Death Cafes and have never failed to be surprised at the intimacy that develops between the participants. The topics that come up for discussion are always different. People have talked about how they cannot discuss their life limiting illness with their families, their vigil sitting with a dying parent. Suicide is sometimes discussed—either their own thoughts about it or their feelings when a loved one has contemplated it.

Often people working in the death industry will attend a Death Cafe, so the details of what actually happens to the bones in the crematorium were discussed at one meeting. In another Death Cafe a woman who made shrouds told us how she tested them. The possibilities are endless of what discussions take place.

When I read through the poems in *The Black River* the range and breadth of the poems reminded me so much of Death Cafes. Although all the poems are concerned with death and dying, the differences in emotion and subject matter are vast. They generated emotions in me similar to the feelings I have experienced at a Death Cafe. There was pain, beauty, interest and sadness. The poems invite us to engage with our emotions, confront our realities, and explore the complexities of the human experience. They lead us to find solace, understanding, and connection— broadening our perspectives and enriching our lives.

Having an open conversation about death and dying is a transformative experience. It can foster connection, understanding and even promote healing. The act of publishing these poems aligns with the philosophy of Death Cafe—that discussing death and dying more openly lessens the taboo, and the innate fear that bringing these topics out in the open will kill you! Instead it enhances the time we have left and in the words of Jon Underwood "helps us make the most of our finite life."

—Susan Barsky Reid
Media Representative and Administrator
Death Cafe
https://deathcafe.com

A Black River Journey
by Deirdre Pulgram-Arthen

When both of my parents died in 2020, under very different circumstances but just two and a half months apart, I found myself floating in space. Despite having performed funerals and sacred rituals around death for over 30 years, being certified as a Death Midwife, and accompanying friends whom I love on their death journey, I was set adrift by the deeply emotional experience of losing these two of my dearest ones so close together. This volume would have been of great help to me then as I tried to come to terms with their absence from my life, and also as I worked with my family to create a ritual of remembrance and celebration for all of us who loved them.

I am honored to have been offered the opportunity to bring together this volume of new poems from around the world, to offer words of solace, commiseration, perspective and hope to others who are grieving. These are not the poems that we already know and love, but fresh voices from a variety of cultures, perspectives and religions which touched me, and which I hope, as a collection, will add richness to the available literature at a time when we need it most. We all experience death in our lives and each time it brings us something new. Whether this time you are angry or bereft, confused or resolute, lost or awakened, there is something here for you. Whether you have lost a parent or a child, a friend or a pet, something in this volume speaks to the experience of that kind of loss for someone else, in very personal terms, with no assumption that your loss will feel the same way.

The Black River is divided into four sections to reflect the process we move through at the end of life—from dying, into death; and then, for the survivors, entering the turmoil of remaining; followed by the journey forward, whatever shape that takes. There are poems for personal reflection and poems that are marked as lending themselves to ritual use. I can imagine opening the book as I sit with someone in hospice and quietly reading to myself, or finding something to read aloud to the dying person or others in the room. I can equally imagine myself as a ritual celebrant in a room or a circle of grieving community members, holding the book and reading something that will open their hearts and ease their spirits. And I can imagine coming home, after the burial of someone I love, after the crowd has gone and the casserole dishes are washed up and put away, to read something that will help me sleep that night.

Reading these poems over and over again as I worked to finalize what would be included, and then again to sort them into sections, and then yet again to index them according to relationships and themes, I have come to know them well and deeply appreciate their honesty and beauty. The poets here are brave in their sharing, and that can encourage us to be brave in our true emotional experience around death.

—*Deirdre Pulgram-Arthen*
Editor

Table of Contents
The Black River: Death Poems

Dying

Change Comes to All Things
by Steve Trombulak

Today my prayer is this:

As loss comes to all things,
May I gain wisdom in the places
made vacant by loss.

As departure comes to all things,
May I find joy in each new arrival.

As failure comes to all things,
May I see the successes that
the failures reveal.

As sickness comes to all things,
May I work to strengthen health
in all beings.

As darkness comes to all things,
May I train my senses to seek out
the light.

As cold comes to all things,
May I embrace it as the state from which
warmth begins.

As uncertainty comes to all things,
May I learn from all the possibilities
that uncertainty allows.

As age comes to all things,
May I honor the journey from infant
to elder.

As death comes to all things,
May I allow each passing to re-awaken
my joy in each birth.

As decay comes to all things,
May I use all the freed elements
to build anew.

Today my prayer is this:

As change comes to all things,
May I make each change
a new beginning.

The Iron Torii
by Janet E. Aalfs

When I place my hand on the iron gate
how happy I am to enter

here in the middle of an ordinary day
a young black bear peers at me

from behind twin trunks of cedar
because no one can prove she is not

Paradise   I say she is
here in the moment we meet

wind picks up my arms below
swaying branches of Mama Oak

how happy I am to dance
this fearless light between

clouds weaving snow atop blue
mountains where we go

because losing you aches deeper
than any grief I know

when I place my hand on the iron gate
how happy I am

merge
by Luther Allen

rotting kelp on clean white cobble
the scrape of rocks pushed away by my boot
layers and layers of blue and grey and forgotten light

i will be leaving this

the wetness   the roundness   the rote of waves
the whoosh of water funneling up a chute
then sliding down the tumbling clefts of gravel

it will go on without me

there is only merge
there is nothing else

a sea otter pops up on the edge of the kelp bed
eyes me
slips under the surface

off shore

by Luther Allen

—for paul, when dying

remember
out in the boat
floating in the wet murmur
the fishing lines
our only anchor
to everything

the water running out to forever

it will take you there
if you let it

passage
by Luther Allen

the crows come

to say goodbye

or to say hello

to covet, to steal

her joy

they fly

into the future

with her

so marvelous

The end of regret
by Carolyn A. Cushing

When you listen to the moon
at year's end, you hear
voices of the dead losing
the world's words one by one:

lawn chair
egg-timer
spatula
hat

They don't need those things now.
The rooms they lived in are emptying,
every day memories unmoored. In the drift,
they forget you were late. Or left early.
Forgot that date. Didn't say.

Your said and unsaid then, don't matter now.
Only the listening to what they still know:
Love
Love
Love
Love
Love
Love
Love
Love
Love
Love
Love

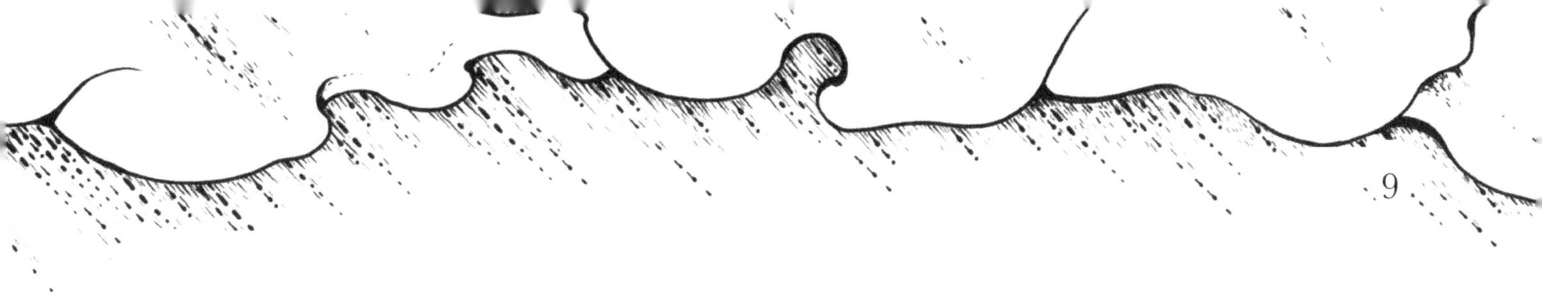

Love
Love
Love
Love
Love
Love
Love
Love

Saturday hike with ventilators
by Katherine Hagopian Berry

I took my children to the lake today
because you might be dying.
Everything moved more slowly,
as if you were there with me,
feet in the shallow, clear water,
lightspray of tanarms splashing,
suturing the sky.

Imagine, your seablue blanket
could be water,
just a summertaste of cold.
Imagine, the light
on your closed eyes
could be the sun.
Imagine, dragonfly
sipping at my shoulder
wings of your IV
tears like a tube in my throat
one hand on my chest
as if I can make it rise and fall
for you.

Paint dark trees against the sunset,
steady well-inked line
of a heart that keeps on beating,
death like a darkshell clam,
burrowing back beneath the sand,
no need to crack it open,
my heart knows you are the pearl,

scar the rapture, future nacre,
hope of more.

Imagine, your seablue blanket
could be water
just a summertaste of cold.
Imagine, the light
on your closed eyes,
could be the sun.
Imagine me
standing like a dragonfly
at your shoulder.
Imagine our laughing,
the bright road home.

All about My Mother
by Geri Gale

Back in the day of father-fire
window lantern left burning
for old souls, coming.
Weak
we waited. Waited.

my mother pickpocket-smooth
replenished our bellies
with shoals of oysters
my mother wicked-shrewd
rehearsed a symphony of lies
partnered cotton and wool
my mother, invisible
iron clavicle, copper-eyed,
strong-armed,
adorned our wrists
with fettered circle-gold
my mother, wing-clipped,
dreamed affinity
back, when, lush, reigned

Ma mere, her crème, her myrrh,
her vale of tears
her pearous hemisphere
in the orchard of her lavished
unmovable bed we lay
under precious sinews of skin,
embryonic air, circle-eight womb
the pure of the pure, purring,
furring, purring.

The Nurse Steels Herself Against the Pediatric Patient's Diagnosis

by Dorinda Wegener

Sometimes emotion has nothing to do with the heart,
but that of the brain by route of the optic nerve, images
from an echo-bubble-study, test positive

carried to and correlated in the occipital lobe, assigned
to memory, myth, or disease, an alchemy.
I'm mainly thinking of red, not of blood,
but anthocyanins—

how, right now, out the conference room window,
a scarlet maple in fall and the cerebrum remembers:
Acer rubrum, having an aspect of crimson for every season
by the protein in its leaves, glycosylated.

And the young patient's mother, in the same said room,
her eyes, not on the tree nor the medical report,
have become almost blind from the mind's processing,
weeps. What remains:

the ever action/reaction of chemical compounds;
the leaves down to a brittle brown once the sugar is spent;
this hole in a heart, and our every need to fill it.

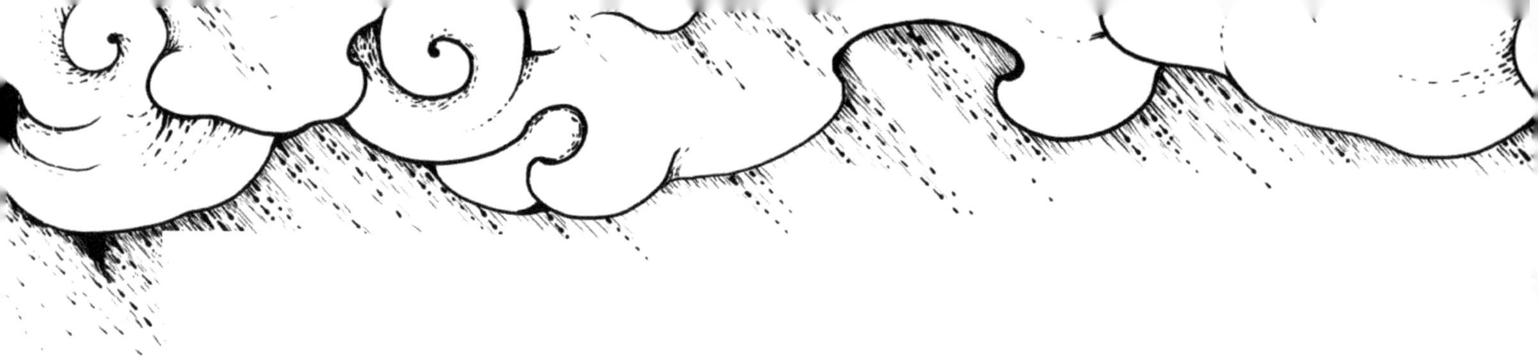

Pause at Sundown
by Joan Hofmann

Then between daylight and dark
When night lowers to flatten, horizon
Rises to surmount the day's drain

A surge is imagined possible
To create with care and fervor
Something extraordinary:

To make something new
Venture into parts unknown!

Then also we think of the forgotten,
The left behind, regrets of past
Settled into our cores, holding place

Grounding us in memory
To gather both gains and losses

And move us, once again renewed
Just enough to breathe into a sigh
And push up from the chair—

Like a turtle lifts her home—
To carry burdens & go on

Lullaby for My Mother
by Rodger Martin

After half-a-century, it's time
to sleep, to turn, hand-in-hand from that corn-
filled summer, to turn from that stroll along the lane,
fields flush with stalk and silk. Time to turn
toward tonight, the stars, and an ancient guitar
strummed by a tall, bearded and balding man
from Italy, stooped like his Appenines
or my Appalachians, his fingering precise
as the mountains' first spring shoots—
tones like the gurgle high above of melted ice
finding its liquid way to the valley
greening below. Time to let go,
lift the tiny finger grasping yours,
those delicate hands you lay on the ivory
of your piano, each key a thrush's call,
dawn and dusk, your singular note
arcing upon the evening velvet,
lingering, lingering, gone.

One in Each Hand
by Susan Marsh

On this day our winter has begun.
Twilight lingers, deepens the gray.
Each slide into dying is unique.
A long road: the only option
is to move forward.

May the birds look into windows
and bring messages of connection.
If you don't see a soaring eagle
a chirping wren will do.
Being there as his life ebbed,
a time of depth and intimacy
profound and filled with light.

Now we wander the hills without purpose.
We are not here to seek closure
there will never be closure
our hands will always reach for him.
Under the silent presence of trees
grief lies alongside gratitude.
Hold one in each palm
and gently close both hands around them.

Memo to the Curious
by Charles A. Perrone

So now I've decided to take
my cavorting to a new level:

I shall commence at once
to go gallivant with gaiety,

tripping about the planet,
around the world, wholly.

It's up to me to plan it.
I am indeed quite able.

To execute the design.
To befriend fellow travelers.
To dress the part smartly.
To address surprise hosts.
To find a suitable end.

And mostly to expire with dignity
on the date indicated on the label.

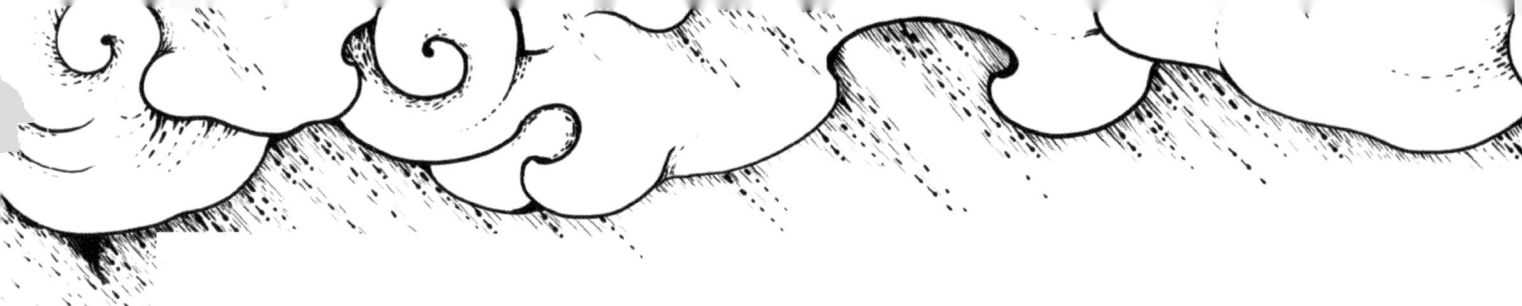

this is the end
by k pihl

there is no time in hospice

the light never changes
the sounds beyond the door never stop

it has been hours, days
no time has passed at all

he is still
under thin hospital sheets
a blanket knitted by a volunteer
sometimes he moans, groans
keens

this is the end

i wake up in the uncomfortable chair
dragged beside his bed
disoriented
a vibrant dream dissolving around me
quiet beeping
a rasping cough from tired lungs
soft fluorescent light pours over us
my legs are numb

heart too
i have never been good at feeling
i feel too much
and somehow not enough

it is 2 am
the clock says 8:30
as if it mattered
as if anything mattered but
the subtle rise and fall
of his chest

there is no end in sight

the tv plays smooth jazz
his favorite
constantly
i want to tear it from the wall
smash it until it becomes punk rock
something i can scream to

he moans, coughs
nurses drift in and out
friendly and faceless

i am faceless too

my grief tucked away
in the deepest part of me
where the light doesn't reach
where the pain doesn't register

this is the end
there is no end in sight

Lingering
by Yehudit Silverman

Soft blanket
hard choices
my dying father's body
stretched thin, translucent

Heart giving way
memories intact

One strawberry
in a vodka tonic

Bells echoing
down a ski mountain

his head out the train window
deep breath

Now an oxygen tank
sets a rhythmic tone
to these final days

He says he wants
a quicksilver ending
the trail of a jet taking off

But instead
lingering
fighting
fists out

The Unwinding
by Rhett Watts

To unwind: to come to the end of a thing such as
the end of a piece of string. Or to be
wound down like the pendulum of a grandfather clock.
The dancing ballerina in a music box, stopped.

To come undone as shoelaces do,
as I have come undone. A jelly roll unrolled.
All my neat knowings unraveled through the labyrinth.
A top wobbling, teetering with grief's inertia.

Fishing line from the rod, hair from the curler,
thread from the spool unwinds as do investments,
marriages. Also, Summer from Spring and our
individual karma, the collagen fibers in our skin.

To unwind: relax, loosen. Take a load off.
Eased up a bit, I may mellow. Slacken, an apple
fallen or leaf floated off its tree. If not at rest,
at least at ease.

Flight Path
by Laura Rodley

Nothing but pinions holding me
to this earth, the thrill of flight,
swooping, green of leaf and blue of sky,
and, oh, the landing, the taking off.
Nothing but air between each breath,
the timing chain of my heart,
the pistons of aorta chugging,
heard only through amplification;
what of my own anvils that pick up
their insistent incessant necessary thrum,
what of my own heart longing for more.
Nothing but rushing of wind between each feather,
how staying aloft is not a miracle to me
only the two-legged walking below, peering up.
I know where I am going, the longing pulls me.
Snow on my wings I keep flying.
Snow on my wings I left it too late.
Snow on my wings I huddle.
Snow on my wings I wait till morning.
What rafters above me, the bulbous clouds,
what oceans below me, the rivers, lakes,
what plenitude I devour, sumac seeds, rosehips,
what succor I keep seeking, swallowing
my own body weight ten times over.
So hot I stayed too long.
So quick the cold weather, I got confused.
So fast the frost, I spun home, too few of us,
so green the trees, saying, it's not time yet, but it is.
So generous the wind when I do not know the word.

So swift the currents when I know nothing but flight.
So soft the clouds when I bump into them, keening,
so hard the tree branch where I spend my night.
Echos through my feathers sing me the longest song,
a breeze of chimes I've heard since first flight.
I huddled near my nest, looking lost on the ground,
but, in truth, I have never been lost, I can always hear you.
I have never been lost, I can always hear you,
I have never been alone, I can always hear you,
I never ceased flying, the chimes singing to me,
I can never tell you how glorious you are, my beloved.
Soon I will leave you but I don't know when that will be.
I will take my last flight without knowing its leap.
Like my feathers, I was born with this imprint of leaving.
Like my longing that steers me, my leaving has always been before me.
I've been flying towards it all my life,
soaring into and through eternity since I pecked out of the egg.
And back again, I always come back, this imprint of leaving upon me.
Until I leave again, without knowing.
I know nothing of hope, but everything of flight.

The Road
by Georgia Gojmerac-Leiner

My friend, the road behind me
is longer than the road ahead.
Each day, each season, each year
I need less and less--
less clutter, fewer purchases, fewer disputations;
and more contentment with what I already have.
I live without fear of what will come
in sincerity of my faith. Though,
when fear comes I process it as bitter herbs.
I pray and pray, and somehow
out of the darkness
comes hope in the form of the moon rising,
aligning with Venus;
or in a sunburst;
or simply in the feel of the smooth oak floor
my feet touch as I ease myself out of bed,
making certain
that I am steady and ready
for the road ahead.
When I die I will experience an ecstasy
which I will not live to tell.

o take me night
by Joe Webster

o take me night
i am not ready
but i will go with you
whip me up into your wind
scatter me among the stars
my bones to the moon
my heart to the sun
my soul to interstellar space
take me to the far away
the o so close
bring me to my constant companion
my shadow twin
the breath on my neck at midnight
the sweat on my back at noon
is it so strange
i would want to go
and join those
who are already there?

Minuet with Death
by Joe Webster

Death takes my hand.
we bow, courteously.
they are splendid
in their shimmering
rich ebony brocade.
as we turn in pleasant angles
Death smiles, and
whispers to me in
a silky enticing tone
"you know this dance will end"
i nod in agreement, the
chandeliers and violas
leaving me breathless
and we step
without speaking the room
candlelit and close
not unlike a tomb
but Death is reassuring
as they guide me
in the dance
that weaves me through
the wavering shadows
in stately grace
and perfect form

Elogia a Un Viejo Más
por Amelia Díaz Ettinger

Tenías hormigas en los pies, por eso viajabas, pero el reloj
marcaba tus horas.
Agitabas a todos que fueran contigo a la Madre Patria,
no sabías que ya ahí estabas.

"Que mi vida se apaga," cantabas sin son con una
descascarada guitarra española.
La guitarra que era lo que tu ansiabas, una condenación,
la simplicidad negada.

Español, españolito, España, pero eras criollo como el
pan de agua.
No se por qué no derramé ni una lágrima,

"para que nunca amanezca". Pero ya han habido
centenares de amaneceres
y no estás más cerca de ser lo que no eres.

The Long Goodbye
by Betsy Guttmacher

Tell your legs how much you love them
kiss kneecaps, gristle, ankle and thigh
to roam is to sing, to whistle out unexplained

Farewell arms, pushing away water, cutting air
plowing, flailing, side-slung and humming
what we hold animates us, countless embraces

So long fine fingertips, all the micro slices
healed without bandages, so many miracles
twisting our hair, entering a thousand forests

And feet, the great conductors, tapping
a mirror of Morse code to fellow strangers
all across the globe, carrying the same load

Good brain and your rivulets, a terrine, a quiver
another day, another map, all this conquest
only to drain, absorbed by sand, picked at by gulls

Dear mysterious heart, we will miss you the most
may your efforts flutter in the hand of another
berry picker, whisperer in acres of lupine

Knots
by Adria Libolt

Mom taught me about varieties of knots,
how they form without bidding,
appear on shoes during a run

I use the basic bow for strings
the double for long laces
avoid tripping over loose ends.

Later her language muddled
garbled words twisted,   dangled   fewer and softer,
bleeding together   tangled, left undone mid   sentence,

giving up attempts to find the thief of speech, I sense
Leviathan stealth swimming, sweeping so close, silent
teeth sinking in, I need to blame a predator, praying, no please

I jog where boaters on harbor's docks
use the clove hitch for temporary mooring
before tying serious figure eights

to keep boats secure and anchored,
ropes from unwinding,
lapping at gentle waves,

boats nod and smile
names like pier spirits, *Resolution* and *Elision*,
storm-confident in ties that bind

My throat's knots like swelling tides

clutch, form lumps, loosen, unravel
swallowing back brine.

securing words futile, my lament of lost
language mourning now, the worst time
aware of decline.

released from knowing, free from tangled speech
peace, my eyes dry well before the service
when she let go.

November 30th, 11:45 PM Central Time
by Charlotte Eulette

November 30th, 11:45 PM Central Time
does not escape me, and now *you,*
for what to do
when the one you're with, is dying.

As they lay before you,
reclined, facing southbound on Lake Shore Drive
somewhat watching the traffic from their 26th floor,
high-rise apartment window they,
will pant in a rapid Yoga Lion's Breath *ha, ha, ha, ha.*
Time speeds up and slows down together and all at once.
At a certain point you will sense when
not to sit too close to them,
not hold their hand or hover over them.
Don't talk with them. Stay quiet and listen to their breath.
If it's night, turned down the lights to dim.
If it's morning, don't close the curtains.
Stay back.

These are good things:
They are doing the work to accomplish
the task of their dying.
You by their side and back a little visible.
No obstacles between you and them.
Stay with that.
The difficult stuff has passed.
Your hours bedside tending to their dying dance of…
touching,
cleansing, redressing,

carrying and laying them back down…
making sure *this one* won't choke on what's brought up.
Not *this one*, not on your life.

After they've fully taken the time to talk
with those on the other side
in a language resembling speech,
their breathing ritual will resume.
No more retching only metronome breathing,
Times come, slowly fingers and toes turn blue.
They might try to sit up a few times to release,
unhook themselves from their bodies,
only to give way, lie back down again
and resume their breathing,
now sounding like a lullaby for you.
The room fills with a transporting essence.
They'll exhale. One exhale, no bigger or smaller
than those that came before,
but this one will have a drum sound-feel.
The one   last   beat,
your tuned-in heart will know before you do.
Come nearer, congratulate them.
Move your hand over their face and close
the lids of their downcast eyes.
You are the closest to their death,
like a baby being born only going the other way.
You've sent them off good, back to whence they came,
back to their familial waters.
Go over their body and straighten their limbs nice and smooth.
Do so before they become stiff
from resting blood and vanished life source.
Button the nightdress.

Pull up the white sheet, fold to show lace and lay their hands on top.
Time has come for you
to go to the living room, to open up that decade-waiting bottle of port
sitting on the shiny brass cocktail cart and pour yourself an ample shot.
Think of nothing else.

Those who will fetch her for what follows will come soon enough.
For now—toast.
Feel the port bathing your parched lips and warming your throat.
Drink and pay it mind.

Here Is My Home. Here Bury My Bones.
by Aby Kaupang

Here is my home. Here bury my bones
among the Allard's, Butler's, Chedsey's,
Coyte's, Hendrickson's, Holsinger's, Ketchum's,
Riddle's, Wamsley's and Wattenberger's.
Among the un-named Utes, trappers, miners,
travelers, ranchers, frontiersmen and thieves.

Bury my bones in the shadow of Mount Pinkham
proud standard of my great great great grandfather
the Canadian James O. Pinkham, who, in 1874
passed through for minerals yet stayed his years.

Here in the high mountain basin
is my home among North Park ranchers. Here we winter
in zero's,
befriend the relentless drifts, the snows that embrace
our cabins as a mother swaddles her babe
and here, where in fall, just as a sow licks her calf
so the wind roughs at the grain.

Here, the sublime spectacle, woven—
Home.
Bones.

of the high plains and the
wetlands weaving creeks, rivers, branches, marshes,
ditches too,
here, bury my bones.

أقدامٌ تسبق الفجر

رمزي سالم

إلى أين يأخذنا هذا الفجرُ
إلى أَيٍّ قَدَرٍ يرمي بنا هذا الضجرُ
هل إلى نهايةٍ تليق بنا
نزرع الطرقات ياسمينا
أم إلى هجرة المستحيل
تَتَبدَّلُ أسماؤنا بالعويل
أَمْ إلى غيابات الجُبّ
نقتات على مذكرات الحُبّ
لا مسار لخطى أقدامنا
فهي ترى السراب وكأنه أمامنا
وتسعى إلى ما بعده وما بَعدَنَا

تسبقنا أقدامنا
وكأنها دليل أقدارنا
وكأنها ترنيمة أرواحنا
تفرش لنا أكفاننا
تبيع لنا أحلامنا
تتاجر بها وذكرياتنا
تسبقنا وتهرب منا
تهرب من سطوة أيامنا
ومن جرأة خيالاتنا
وصخب أمعائنا
وتقودنا إلى حتفنا

كيف لها أن تدلّنا على أسمائنا
في أول ليلةٍ تحت سَقْفِ سمائنا
وآخر لحنٍ يرتعش على أوتار أعمارنا
عندما يلتهم الصدأ هياكل أجسادنا
وتنخر الريح الرطبة فراغ عظامنا

ويصير ورق الصفصاف وشاحًا لرقابنا
ويشيّد الحمامُ عُشه فوق تضاريسنا
يربي صغاره في تجاويف ضلوعنا
ويترعرع الياسمين في أعماق قلوبنا

هل تدلنا علينا وعلى أحبابنا
من تجذر رحيق عطرهم في أعناقنا
وتردد صدى ضحكاتهم في صدورنا
وانعكست صورهم على وجوهنا
هل تدلنا علينا وعلى مأساتنا
على تردد وحِدَّة صدى آهاتنا
على مواساة الظل في وحدتنا
على قهرنا ودموعنا في دعواتنا
وحنيننا إلى لحظة ولادتنا
وآخر نجوانا قبل صعودنا

سأنام، لعل قلبي يكبر ويصير غيمة
يسافر صوتي من خلالها مثل نغمة
تأخذنا في فجر جديد إلى وجهة قديمة
نقيم فيها جنازة لزرقة البحر الساحرة
وجنازة لخضرة الصفصاف المهاجرة
وملايين الجنازات الأخرى للدماء الثائرة
سألملم شتات ذرات الهواء المتآمرة
أكدسها في حقائب الذاكرة
وأرمي بها في جوف الباخرة
لعلها تسبق الفجر وأقدامنا الحائرة
تأخذنا إلى قَدْرٍ جديدٍ وحياة زاهرة

Funerary prayers
by H. Byron Ballard

You have come to the end of this pathway
In a journey to which we bear witness.
You have come to the end of a pathway
That is barred with a gate and a door.
May this door open swiftly and silently.
May this gate give you
a moment's grace
A pause in which to rest your spirit
before you venture through.
We stand here with you, as your companions,
As your family, for you are beloved.
But, for now, we must remain here.
We can not go with you to this old land.
Not yet.
For you will see the Ancestors.
You will see the Beloved Dead.
You will walk among the Divine Beings
That guide and nurture us all.
You go to dwell in the lands
Of summer and of apples
where we dance,
forever youthful, forever free.
Now
We hear the music in the mist
The drums that echo our sad hearts.
We see your bright eyes and your smile.
And so we open the gate

We push back the door
We hold the gate open
We glance through the doorway
And with love and grief and wonder
We watch you walk through.
Hail the Traveler!
All those remembered in love, in honor,
Live on.
Farewell, o best loved,
O fairest,

Farewell.

Death

Songs of the Dead and Dying
by Mary Brancaccio

Young eye, what do you see
when you look through the lace
of a dead fan coral?

Azure sky, purple cloud pregnant with rain
cobalt of deep current, green curl of shallow wave
stained glass in the church
where my father was waked:
colors broken, rewoven
light bleeding through.

Every tear is a tiny womb
that carries a child of grief.

All that is, all that was
is transforming
evolving, adapting

becoming petal

becoming breast

becoming cup

becoming boat

becoming fire

becoming smoke.

The lost speak in the vireo's voice
their light shining like silver fronds
blessed by morning sun, they dance
in orchid scent, in plumeria, they send
dreams: I am flying like a frigate bird
above an ocean of endless waves, I am
swimming in a cloud of parrotfish
inside a cradling sea.

The dying whisper through osprey's bone
in the femur of goat
in conch's cracked shell
in coconut husk, in ding
of stone on the ironshore:

fragile fragile fragile

you have forgotten how fragile you are.

The dead ask, how will you walk through the world

if you close your ears to our song?
How can you live without our grace?

The dead and dying say,
you will never heal alone.
Until you dismantle
the wall around your heart
your mourning will be an empty belly

always hungry

always devouring.

You Could Tell Yourself
by Zeina Azzam

You could tell yourself almost anything.
That when you look at your mother
on her deathbed you say well, she had a full life.
You see that her diaphragm is no longer rising
from a sacrum once rife with life
and it makes you wonder about her final breath,
is it still in the room and can you breathe it in too,
carry it in your veins.
You know that her favorite blouse is scissored open
in the back for easy dressing and it makes you consider
which of your own clothes you will die in,
which ones will be given away to strangers.
You could tell yourself that these are ephemeral things,
that living to the fullest is what is important
and then you ask, what does that mean.
There are songs on the shelf that make your tears flow,
books that tell of journeys toward an inner heaven
or one beyond. There are the good deeds that maybe
made someone's life better. Then there is this love
that overwhelms you, for her, for your brother
who, with you, is the only one left, for your children
who you are terrified might also die before you.
It sits heavily like the thick roots of an old tree,
its high branches and leaves trying to fly….
You want to believe this love has a lightness
like that too, that it will fly and last beyond
your physical body and hers, that people remember
the dead this way despite the dark absence.
You could believe it. And then you think

of your mother on her deathbed and you realize
you do. That nothing is as important as loving,
even if you cannot touch your loved ones after they die.
You could then tell yourself that there are unnamable,
invisible hands that will continue to open, close,
flutter like leaves between you and your mother
and that maybe with the photographs
and the memories that come when you close your eyes,
that this is really all there is.

Succession
by Pamela Hobart Carter

When you come home
your mother will be silent
like a queen in a new fairy tale.

In once-upon-a-time, you heard her,
her sounds the first to ever greet
your ears. You grew to her voice,
her counsel guided you.
Perhaps a vibration pings
against, or within, a secret recess,
which you will rediscover
if only everything else stills,
or if you sit quietly enough.

Her throne reminds you of succession,
of evolution, in its inevitable emptiness.

You might choose it for yourself
and picture how she dropped her shoes
to curl her stocking feet under her on the cushion.
You might take up the paperback
left on the spot, and riffle through it
hopeful for a pressed four-leafed clover,
some further evidence of resonance.

When the Tall Grass has been Bleached and Dyed to the Paleness of November

by Tommy Twilite

when the harvest has come and gone

when the number of boats on the river is one

when the angle of the sun
slaps the horizon in your eyes

when green is a memory of sweetness
amongst a hundred shades of brown

when day is a brief intrusion
and night is winning

when bugs are no longer a threat

when a dirt road is your only friend

when frogs burrow in to hide

when sky glows blue against purple mountains

when trees are just trees

when the hawk shows her white underwing

when the truth lies in autumn afternoons

when it is serenity before December
for one blessed day

when the cornstalk rustles its dry whisper
to the night wind

then I will be here
waiting for you

The Beautiful Death
by Tommy Twilite

spirals to earth
something poetic
a brightly colored biplane
streaming fire
plumes of darkness
too beautiful to watch

this final dance
is the opera
she always wished to write
one day in the life
one night of love
now it is finished

she raises her hand
to wave goodbye
her gown flutters in the breeze
sheets billow on the clothesline
this is the reckoning
for her acrobatic airshow
this is the song
she had to sing

How Does One Survive
by Candace R. Curran

or two survive the making ready for
release   arms open the you and I
breaking   the way a spirit will
vanish from its shell

Where does it go?

If tears could bring you back
perhaps there would be no death
if weeping filled the ocean   wouldn’t we
swim within its hollow womb

Did I ever tell you…I never learned to swim.

Treasure and debris wash and tumble
and you have gone and fallen   flawless
into the red wine sea   clever in its
attempt to drown sorrows

How can I blame you….how do I forgive?

Family

by Curt G. Curtin

—for Eleanor

All through the ice of winter she lay
fragile and light as a Meissen figurine
wrapped within her family's embrace,
her bright chemise a slash of springtime
color amid pale sheets, dark eyes
alive when one of her own came in.

Mother of seven, grandmother of thirteen,
she didn't want to leave a one of these—
not now, not even from this breathless bed
where every day and every night she
struggled for a little air, waiting for one
of her own to appear at the bedroom door.

Years before, the third of seven died, and
everyone knew he never left her grieving eyes;
and every other child, in their own light,
she held them in her eyes as if her sight—
stronger than all the mistakes that they
could make—would bring them safely home.

And there they came, loving sons and daughters
in attendance every day. "Whatever she wants
is what we'll do;" and round the clock and
turn by turn she never was alone at home,
and the strength was in their eyes this time
and she relied on their determined care.

Nobody's arms are stronger than time.
Hands that stroked her hair, and lips that
kissed her in the night, they always knew
their energy could not diminish dying;
each touch was only to delay the leaving, and
every kiss a godspeed with the lips and grieving.

The End—If I Could Write It
by D. Dina Friedman

Someone
is bending
over me

as if
I'm about
to die

or, perhaps,
already dead.
They're aching

for the word
to close a conversation
never opened

while I'm lying
in my final fuzz,
their face veiled

in the blur.
I try to wavelength
a message

though I barely feel
the small squeeze of heat
through their damp fingers.

It's okay. Whoever you are.
Whatever the problem.
I forgive you.

Para mi Óbito
por Amelia Díaz Ettinger

Cuando llegue mi calaverita
a buscarme, que me dé un beso,
y que baile una plena, y me llene
de flores silvestres el pecho.

Le pido a esa santa muerte
que grite mi nombre,
para que brinden las aves
con los lagartos de mis deseos.

Que las tortugas del océano,
y hasta el pobre cemento, recuerden
la corta sombra de mi cuerpo.

Porque como dice Mary Oliver,
—No solo quiero haber
visitado por un tiempo.

Bury Me in Motherhood
by Betsy Guttmacher

wash my gone body
in the hum of school pick-ups

the raucous cacophony
of echoey old gyms

wrap me in the heat
of my roaming children

enfold me in a muslin of
soft elbows and chins

please, big sky, let me be
forever nestled, at home

with endless kin, porch
warm sunlight, blue wind

War
by Wallace Fong

We are not strangers to war,
but how it feels this time
I don't know what to do,
I have no place to go,
I cannot pull myself up.
I cannot find the words,
even the words to talk
to myself.

The Many Ways to Drown
by Suzanne S. Rancourt

This 1st responder will carry you forever
the air bubbles gasping from Dog Days river muck
will make him vomit for years to come. He will never again
split the breast of a Christmas or Thanksgiving turkey
without feeling your green 8 year old ribs crack
from adrenaline fired chest compressions. He will never
allow his own children near the river or lake or pool
again, and they will rebel – scream adolescent hate at him
hurl dejection glaringly, stand lily white
on the outer side of the chain link fence while their friends,
friend's parents and school mates flutter kick
and bob between lifeguard whistles, their arms floundering.
He will not be able to save his own children
from misconceptions, fallacies, fake news, propaganda or
risk-driven misunderstandings communicated
by his own grief and what ifs – what if
they had searched there first? What if
someone had noticed the boy's absence sooner? What if
tell me, what if,
the loss of all children was mourned equally?
What if this river's death did not pull him back into the humidity
that gags him still as still
as lifeless children
in a man's arms – a father's arms? How
do we protect from this?
Keep safe.
Keep clean.
How can a man wash clean from this kind of self inflicted
failure when his arms still carry the weighted truth?

He did everything he could and still
it was not enough.

Shon's Bend

by Sharon A. Harmon

—for my beloved son

Searching both ends of the river
running rampant in twisting loops,
we searched woodsy trails
to no avail.

Four-wheeled on a deep
rutted road hoping to
lead to a place in the bend
named for you.

Foolish in our frenzy to find it
to not find it knowing it was named
and meant something to someone
whom I believed did little
to care for your leaving.

We met a fisherman who knew all
the nooks and crannies of the silver
serpent river, sent us back to a path we had
missed, past McKenzie's Pool and bear right.

As we reached the bend
a large falcon rose
from the trees like a phoenix
rising, it was a sign to me.
You always loved birds.

I gazed toward the river at an
official sign, on a tree
bearing your name.
Smooth rocks and blue water
eased downstream.

You were by my side
swaying on the current.

Dawn Watch

by Caitlín Matthews

—on my mother's passing

Two birds fly up in the dawning
As the darkness turns to gold,
Clouds pass south to the rising tide
Like argosies of old.

With scarce a breath to fill her sails,
She lies in the harbour slack;
Enduring the roll of the petulant shoal,
She waits for the wind to back.

As day dawns pure, night's peace slips out,
The bustle of life speeds on.
Becalmed in a mist that hugs the shore,
Her colours flame, fade, and are gone.

Those who sleep with dread to rise,
Dream fast of the voyage to come.
For the chart tells not where the barque must steer,
Nor how deep the lead might plumb.

By unseen star her chart is set,
To unknown seas she steers.
Her goal, desire of shores long-dreamed,
Her freight, the untold years.

The sun comes up with crown of gold;
Her captain cries, 'All hands!'
Two birds as pilots clear the clouds
As she sails to distant lands.

Wet Sand
by Heather Pankl

When we meet death and that long preparation—
gathering, sorting, sifting—
recedes like the wave going back to sea,
leaving us standing on an unknown shore,
feet sinking into wet sand,
face away from the ocean
after a lifetime gazing across its wondrous depths,
trying to make out the shapes of distant continents,
now all we are is being—
no hidden acorn stashes to find
or columns of numbers to add up
to figure out which bills to pay
and which to leave another month.
There is no other month.
Time has stopped and started, like a watch
crown spinning with no purchase,
sand timer ever shaking.
We meet, alone, in the in between space
where stillness and movement become one
and sink together softly,
no longer needing to swim.

Sea Burial

by Angela (Angie) Trudell Vasquez

Backpacks, a week of groceries, no hospital
for 200 miles, no wheels, I survived –

on the island where once in a clearing
we came upon an animal meeting,
hooves and feathers flee, mass exodus.

There lies part of me, my man –
wedged beneath blinding white rocks.

Body whispers, blood and rot.

Until sediment slides down
the fifteen-foot cliff back to the sea.

Campfire ashes circle the base.

Where pelicans preen and eagles train
to feed, is our born too early zygote.

My two became one.

Female island ghosts told me
sit in the water let life wash out and back
cool stone slabs your throne. We know.

A sea burial. A hollow tree.
Limestone markers.

your poem
by k pihl

your poem started with anticipation
and joy
with two blue lines on a thin white stick

it started with smiles
and nausea
and tiny socks
with plans
and scribbles of names on scraps of paper
with a belly that had just started to grow

i thought your poem would be seven months longer
that there would be
blurry photos of a uterus
a heartbeat
a nursery
contractions

but when i sat down to write
what came out was
blood
and cramps
and a trip to the ER
where you fell away like the leaves in october
when you were going to emerge

so your poem ended early
with you the size of a sesame seed
with words as heavy as my heart

Harpist's Hands
by Rhett Watts

At the appointed time in the Bartok piece,
the concert harp leans back into the arms,
the body of the harpist where it rests
straddled like a cello or child in her lap.

Her fingers weave sound. Unseen are the open-fingered
gloves like the ones that boxers wear in training.
She wears hers to protect against the skin-splitting pluck
of flesh on steel strings.

Now, there is only the music descending on
a stairway of scales. Staggered,
she waits to still vibrating strings, pounce on notes—
a hand over an open mouth.

In the last movement, she releases the harp
in one continuous movement away from her.
Stands it upright, weighty, wood on wooden boards.
This is how I would release you.

Sy the Aesthete
by Dan Close

he brought honey, apples,

all good things

brought peace to warring parties

certitude to those who struggled

he was the placid river

the sighing of the wind in the pines

brightness white clouds

gentle rains
gladness

all these things were happy in him

he never met a day he didn't like.

And he knew how to leave when it was time to leave

he did not beg for life

but simply went

when it was time

Blood Moon
by Meg Weston

In early dark, the moon was full
when I walked the dogs this night after
the clocks turned back; we were adjusting
to new times. The searchlight in the sky
interrogated the ragged outlines of my grief.
Planets hung low. A year ago, the moon
turned red, your heart stilled
by a lethal dart—fentanyl.

Eclipsed again, by early morning I watched
the moon's crescent fade into a pale red scream;
I hung on to see a sliver of your smile like a treed
Cheshire cat,
until the moon fell into earth's shadow, stopping time,
while I walked through a forest of memories,
this lunar orb of you, watching over me.

The Blood Moon Tolls
by Meg Weston

On the day of the blood moon eclipse,
we awakened to a morning hymn of waves

pounding rocks outside the rented cabin.
We visited a bell foundry that day,

watched flames liquifying bronze bars
poured into molds cast of sand,

transfiguring essence into sound—
bronze bells and wind chimes.

At sunset, watched the full moon rise
over an expanse of yawning sea.

Before the eclipse,
we held hands.

Before the darkness came,
moonlight shimmered on the waves.

Before the death-knell;
Before the call that came around eight;

Before the words: Overdose. Heroin. Fentanyl.
Before red blood congealed in blue-black veins.

Long before this occultation, a rising swell of opioids,
swept in its wake a hundred thousand lives that year.

We wept and lay awake all night staring at the ceiling
while the earth's shadow stole the moon, until

just a sliver remained illuminated by the sun. Red light
of a thousand sunsets cast upon its lunar surface.

Earth's orbit followed its course, eclipsed the moon
in penumbra. Earth's specter lengthening its red light
umbra.

The longest eclipse of our century,
the longest shadow.

The Sign Reads: Prophesies Are Coming True
by Meg Weston

The moon and Mars peered through sixty-foot
pines in night's dark poetry.

Something wild awakened me—
screeching coyotes pouncing on prey?
the moon appeared as olivine crystals glowing gold

from a meteor's crash. The largest meteor to hit the earth
in Namibia heated sand so hot it fused into blown glass—

yellow orbs in the desert—visits from the stars—
my startled eyes open—the dream doctor's voice lingers-

—she is on the final elevator ride down—

my friend stands as tall as the king's pines, irreverent
as a circus of squirrels launching from delicate limbs,

full of the truth only a true friend can tell us.
she's been by my side for decades of tangled travels,
now at the end of her journey—

will she stay with me as the glimmering magneto-
rotational swirl around the black hole in my galaxy?

death rode in
by k pihl

death rode in
on a white hospital bed
pale
and drawn
a rattle in wet lungs

he was in no rush
there was no hurry
he would have my grandfather in the end
so
we breathed deep
felt our hearts beat in our chests
and
when we were ready
he took my grandfather's hand
on top of thin sheets
and escorted him from this place.

people say death is cruel
he takes and takes
with no discretion, no regard

but this is true too:
when you leave this life
it will never be alone
death will ride with you
until the end of the line

he sat with us
with those that loved my grandfather most
gathered around his frail body

standing vigil
beside a life so well-lived
it was hardly a tragedy at all

Anna

by Elaine Reardon

Our handful of homes tuck along
six miles of forest on Bald Mountain.
We call each other— do you have electricity,
do you want some apples?
All of us are more comfortable
in shadowed forest, rather than
being with people for long.

Now it's spring and we listen
to Moss Brook run free. Bears
are awake, followed by frogs.
It's how we tell time passing.
We all grieve for Anna,
the first of us to leave.

How do we say goodbye to a friend?
As a child, Anna began mornings with milk,
Its thickness coated her glass,
straight from the cow.
Could this morning's milking
bring Anna comfort, help
loosen what still ties her here?

Poetry Friends
by Jefferson Navicky

I didn't even know her that well
only bumped into each other
a few times at poetry events.
Press mates, we rolled eyes together
about our disorganized publisher
but always came back to the beauty
of his books and how much we loved
him like a father never present
enough, but one we knew loved us.
The poetry world is filled with
such connection where we see each other
a handful of times a year, congratulations
on your recent publication, have you read,
how's the writing going, we ask each other
like those forced in the outside world to speak
a foreign language who finally for these few
hours return to our mother tongue.
I hadn't even known she was sick,
she seemed so happy at the book festival
last fall. Her memorial at a church
in South Portland next Saturday.
I'll be there.

Deathsong

by Yehudit Silverman

Why do we pray for the dead?

Sing
as body becomes bone?

Are we waiting for something to happen
like the crow
who stands
by the side of the road

Solemn
in his black shroud

I ask
because I do it

Gospel for my best friend
laid out in white
(she would hate it)

Hebrew chants for another

And my father
lying still on the bed
his old eyes
young
just before

I swooped in
with song

Like the crow
I can't help it
something about death
that draws me in
tells me in its own dark voice
what to do

And its choiceless
as the cry of a newborn
still wet with womb

I try with language
to lift the veil
see a little more
than I know

As my mother
hallowed out
takes her last breath

I raise my voice
in gratitude
for this black shrouded
wing tipped
wonder
that we can offer it all up
in song

The bones
the beauty
the breaking apart…

Remaining

Decay
by Steve Trombulak

If I am to embrace life, I must also accept aging.
If I accept aging, I must acknowledge death.
If I acknowledge death, I must yield to decay.

In death, a body does not simply disappear.
Its lifestuff is broken apart and scattered,
transformed and transported to build anew.

All that lives is made of all that died.
All that dies feeds all that will live.
Both part of the indivisible Whole, eternal.

In Defense of Stones

by Janet MacFadyen

For instance, take that stone
by the guard rail over there. One day
it will break down into sand, won't it?
And be mixed with leaves and leached

by water, oh slowly, but for sure?
Then won't a root suck it up with its long
flexible straw, powered by the secret
green lips of the plant? Won't it suck

with all the fierce joy it can muster?
And if the plant were a bean, perhaps I eat
each pod, feeling the rightness of it,
and one day this whole stone will be inside me

and I speak from prior knowledge
of generations of stones lodged in my gall
bladder, the knowledge that I too will be ground
in the dark gizzard of the world.

I chew this notion over and over, how it happens
that I could end up food for a rock
or the rock itself: rigid and grey
and alone. But maybe stones

are just another way of living—
you could say a different style—
and if only we knew how to listen
to such enormous or tiny sounds,

we could hear their low, age-long conversations
at cliff bottoms or along riverbeds;
or feel how they embrace life so fiercely
they batter themselves to bits.

So I wonder, who is the stubborn one here—
the boulder in the field refusing to budge
for anyone, or me in the road,
arguing with myself, refusing to live?

Study of a shoreline
by Joanna Lee

The quiet of a place
that cannot decide
if it wants to be forgotten
will always breathe with ghosts

Ghosts of ships that were never put to sea,
with their ring of ghostly hammers
on sullen metal slunk into the rain's
steady echo

Ghosts of the fishermen
who took from these currents
their brothers in sandy pools; ghosts
of lure and line and old bones

In the wet rust of leaf fall, ghosts
of patient towpath oxen
& great weighted bateaus
drug through one canal chamber to the next

Ghosts
of all those boats carried,
from the city and back to her;
ghosts of a future that was to meet them at the docks

Ghosts, too, of iron and creosote, of ice blocks
and pickaxes and bibles. You can see their pale hands
when breeze off the river blows the Queen Anne's lace
just so

Ghosts of beginnings, and of hope, tried prayers
in a new tongue, how they grew
into the stale ghosts
of smoke, again and again

Under all, the ghosts of waters that knew this land
like a lover, before the river fell and the bay drew back,
a lament that drips through the long-closed canal locks
like a live thing, remembering

Cemetery Stones in Winter
by Curt G. Curtin
—for Robert

Snow gives them a postcard look,
serene, peaceful.
But we come there for one we know and love,
not for the poetry of snow.
A special presence of mind is what we carry
to that cold place, each one's presence, a
communion.
We speak from a spirit within, and what is spoken
is familiar, of family, a presence that never melts.
We stand in a row and say the words together.

As we leave we see again the postcard scene,
silent coexistence with others' lives, others' losses
among cold stones' community.

My Grandmother Enters the Stage In the Rain
by Georgia Gojmerac-Leiner

I
Like a giant washboard,
the rain-water ridges on the pavement.
I've been watching the wind waver,
like the spindle in my grandmother's hand,
fling the rain on the pavement, abate,
then drive it up again
just as it begins to rush downward:
what I want to write cannot be written.

II
My grandmother, disguised
as a washer woman, comes,
in her faded blacks,
a chunk of soap in one hand,
and a stiff corn cob, her brush in the other.
Have you come to scrub away my grief,
grandmother, or to scrub away the pavement?
Have you come to tell me how the earth feels,
dry or moist,
whether the seeds of grass survive underneath.

III
Someone,
dearer than even you
grandmother, has died.
Is he lonely? Are you playing with him?
I do not call out to you in the rain,
you are deaf.
I would write you a note, but in life
you were illiterate.
Once, trying to open a can of pepper,
you bent and scraped it:
the words “to open, lift here,”
eluded you.
My grief is like that,
a sealed container.
I beat on it,
I read the scriptures
but I cannot turn up
the right exegesis.

Orphan
by Robert Eugene Perry

sitting at the ocean
feeling like an orphan
emptiness engulfing
swallowed in the mourning

sunlight anathematic
clouds bring welcome cover
gulls join in the keening, a
symphonic minor number

heaviness descending
tide is rising higher
desire to surrender
swallow all this water

lay there at the bottom
blissfully forgetting
returning to the Mother
the Ocean's never ending.

Sign Language
by M. Anne Sweet
—for Jo Nelson (1946-2001)

Leaf bones
laid across my shoe
by the wind   her hand –
no small mistake.
She drops leaves   Dylan Thomas at my feet,
tells me
Lorca is the ghost who follows her.

She speaks in bones
left on a hill   beside the well.
I climb her mountain.
Holly and maple wail at my feet.
She speaks in leaves.
Listen –
a single leaf falls
where no tree stands near.

She speaks in a rose gown
at night   beside my bed,
aspen leaves caught in her hair.
She speaks at dawn
caped   red over Olympic peaks –
her smile beaked,
goose feathers fly from loose braids
as she dances   raven
on sandaled feet.

She speaks in signs
left beside the road.
A heron lands in the ditch.
An eagle hunts low on the beach –
I follow –
for three miles her wingtip
fingers my hair.

Poem for the Fourth Child
by Dorinda Wegener

There are many things to consider:
wondrous billow of kitchen curtain,
the blackbirds as they school the sky
against a cloud, the waxwing's bittersweet
tips, or the cells we carry—our medical
imaging. What to do when chromosomes,
spindled apart, nettle instead of pair?
Our mother and father: perspiration pinned.
Their chest cavities all blood quake and grasp
for care. Such perfume went into you—
four legs, four arms, lungs, sinew—prayer.
For cynosure you are a God, and what it is
of God: resin and stardust, covered mirror
a pressed shirt. You are cleaned, then clothed as just
the other day: after the caul and secudines,
after the baptismal, you! Alive
with responsiveness for and before
our eyes, your hands upraised
white flags to the glory, bane in the air.

How the Living Carry The Dead

by Jeevan Bhagwat

We carry them in the early
morning hours,
through the glimmer of dawn
into the world of the living
which they have now left
behind.

Throughout the day they
inhabit us,
move within our bodies
in a weightless desire
to fill their need
for gravity.

Sometimes we see them
in the faces of strangers,
in a smile or gesture
familiar to our eyes
and then, in an instant
they are gone again,
always leaving us with

the wretched heaviness of loss
our hearts must inevitably bear.

At night
we take them with us to bed,
offer prayers to the heavens
and patiently await

their arrival in the spirit
landscape of our dreams,

this is how we carry them

from their past to the present
and into our future,
with every step
we take in grief,
with every strand
of memory,

for that which we bury
our love exhumes.

The Winter Coat

by Sigrun Susan Lane

—in memory of Geoffrey

It was a gift I could give him.
In October he chose a coat that suited him—
the high-tech lining reflected
body heat inward. Heat holding
interior cuffs. A vest that zipped out.
Blue, the color of his eyes.
He figured he had a couple of years
to wear it ---that's what the doctors said.
He was pale and thin, as you might expect.
But that day his spirit was buoyant.

It snowed in December; five inches fell overnight.
He wore the coat sledding with his daughter—
two on a sled raced downhill, screaming with laughter.
They built a crooked snow man
that washed away in the next day's rain.
My son died four months later, in early April.
His wife slowly gave away his shirts, his jeans.
But the coat still hangs in the closet.
His scent gone from the seams.
All the newness still in it.

In the Dark
by Candace R. Curran

After the Funeral
In the night the music box
Playing on its own

Telling the Bees
by KB Ballentine

Do I mention you by name? Tell them
how I lost you? Or do they already know –
your presence already humming in the hive?

This honey-colored day should be gray,
misted and fogged as my dreams.
Or maybe not.

Maybe the sun glides over the sycamores
and sweet gums, flecks the ferns with shade
and shine because your spirit infuses
this place with memories of your laugh,
of your hands – careful and kind.

One gatherer mumbles past, whispering
the tip of my ear. Maybe I shouldn't tell them.

You *are* here.

Last Night My Father Returned
by Janet E. Aalfs

Last night my father returned
books spread on the table
thick rough-edged paper
each cover a different silhouette
this one he pointed for you
it's beautiful
take this one
I could have
reached out my hand
but I knew the wild would flee
like before he died when I found
near his house in a grid of streets
a field not yet erased
where fox kits romped in chicory
leaping at butterflies they shone
from his eyes when I showed
how I stood so still
they did not vanish

With Time
by Subhaga Crystal Bacon

Wind is erasing the hills this morning,
blurring their lines with a white mist
of lifted snow, the northern sky
an imperturbable blue. The turmoil
of air is not its business. I kneel
before Quan Yin, her four arms
hold a lotus, the braided loop of infinity,
and two hands touch in the sign of prayer.
I contemplate the suffering in this world
and ask for relief. It blows like the wind
lifting snow. It sweeps around the earth
like a silk veil, this exhale. In and out,
breath and wind, darkness and light,
living and dying. It goes on with us
and without. These bones settle on the cushion,
in the body, compressing like the rings of trees,
rooted in the neutral, ever changing earth.

For the Widow
by Susan Marsh

You have entered a time of leaving who you were.
Who you will become lies beyond an indistinct horizon.
Breathe. Rest. Listen. Pray.

The way is there and you will come to trust it.
Pain cannot be taken from you but it is shared
by those who care. We feel it with you, now.

Sometimes grief slaps and stabs and washes you
under a wave. You wonder, how can I go on?
Other times small gifts arrive—a stirring sunrise,

an ephemeral blossom on the desert floor.
They will come when you aren't watching
and delight you with surprise.

Gutted

by Yehudit Silverman

I stand in the ocean
seaweed wrapped
consecrated
by whatever words
the waves leave behind

I grow gills
so I can sing
with fish tailed ladies
hovering always
below the surface

The rumble of motorboats
careless laughter
from a water skier in a bikini

She doesn't see the rogue wave in the distance

Disaster on a sunny day
not supposed to happen

My best friend from childhood
called me every year on my birthday
sang a different tune
until one year
no song
just the news
stage four breast cancer

She held her pregnant belly
and asked me,
"What should I do"?

Fish tailed ladies
taught me well -
how to sing with no breath

She kept the baby

Our last summer
as mothers together
children crawling in sand
we walk slowly to the ocean
my friend holding on to me
limping, bandaged,
I pick up a thick strand
of glistening brown seaweed
wrap it around her
gently

Cancer in every bone

Gutted, hairless, "like a newborn newt"
she says laughing

We will always be there
feet sinking in sand
the taste of salt
sacred
on young lips

Because I love
by Carolyn A. Cushing
—After Kathleen Raine's *Amo Ergo Sum*

Because I love
leaf unfurls deep green to drink
radiant sun, day's pilgrim of the sky.

Because I love
oak branch prickled with light
forms acorn, seed of the next season.

Because I love
catbird and crow mix hidden
sweet and sharp among the leaves.

Because I love
the stream is cool where boy and girl
crabwalk the rocks, squeal
 when foaming water hits them.

Because I love
there is rock, eternal
in its breaking.

We live in the shatter.

Because I love in the shatter
I put my rock heart down
by the dark bird dead,
breast pointed to the sky.

Because I love in the shatter
there is a river undammed
rimmed with lace and gold,
all weeds, twinning.

Because I love in the shatter
a nest is made from broken twigs,
some down and twists of trash.

Because I love in the shatter
blackbird, that catbird, larks and a sparrow,
insistent in their song at dawn, break light
out of night, stars fall as we rise
into a day as yet untouched
and tempting us to live,
yes, live, as if we mattered.

For François
by Kate Rex

When the shock diminishes
and his absence gently unravels and spreads itself out,
when his colleagues have returned to work
absorbed in projects he is no longer a part of,
when everyone else has turned back and continued
just a few of you will remain
to absorb it all and adjust.

Your father and his stories will be told by many
A re-construction of him through different eyes
filtered through their love for him
and what he brought to each,
every person will add pieces of themselves.
A reconstruction, but maybe not the essence of the father
you knew.

You will occupy some of his stories,
too close, hard to support at first,
a stiff leather jacket
that will ease with time,
becoming more supple
taking your shape
and wrapping itself carefully around you.

Grief Stones

by Janet E. Aalfs

Grief pulled me down
into a silence so deep
I could only hear it
fully submerged in the sea
as I clapped two stones
whose rhythms pierced my body
until my skin became
the fur of a hungry seal
and I had swallowed a fish
gaping gills to tail
and even slivers of bone
still stuck in my throat
can’t dim
rainbow scales
in heaven’s darkest place
I sing to savor

Grief
by Curt G. Curtin

Perhaps you have entered that infinite space
where only the ache seems real and the rest
like the hum of a distant machine. Voices
follow on padded feet and your smiles
are muffled replies to sympathetic eyes.

Gone, but felt nearby, like a shadow life
of nerves in an amputated leg, and you say,
"Where…?" but that returns you to your
space where only the ache remains, the
hollow center of grief. Even so, voices
reach you there and you answer, lovingly.

Something in you knows that morning comes
after the rites and heavy days are done
and the long bonds of love do not break
   when twisted hard as this.

Coming Home
by Patrick Curry

Burying your ashes
it felt we were returning
          to the Earth
something borrowed,
now back where
          it belonged.

It was almost a relief,
even as my eyes filled
          at the finality
and my hands
have never felt
          so empty.

Losing the Child, Haad Tien, Thailand
by Anne Bergeron

on lithic sand
south china sea
pale green wavelets lick
violet necked cowries
as froth lathers my toes

soft-shelled creatures
shuck their shells
vacant, while I finger
sterile coral littering
this thalassic homeland.

I don't need a chart
to tell me what isn't here
my own chamber
an abandoned carapace
echoing back to me

I smooth my skirt of rainbow colors
bought yesterday at a dusty stall
where the old woman with one eye
smelled sorrow then knelt
and tied silver anklets to my feet.

in the harbor
a fishing junk
hoists one red sail
bow and stern curling
toward the cloudless sky

where whimbrels soar
above simmering currents
and the sun's
strange tentacles
overbrine a warming sea

I scry the future
in these fevered broken waters
with you   my unborn silent heir
then I reef the main mast in requiem
and graft my grief for sails

Forget-Me-Nots
by Victoria Field

A constellation of blue eyes
that cannot look this way

Insistent names calling out
with nothing at all to say

A frilled and speckled counterpane
with no small soul asleep

A dancing, posing prettiness
but no lock of hair to keep

A scattering of loveliness
that won't take shape nor grow

I'll remember you who never were
and can neither come nor go.

The Primitive's Grave Barrow At Avebury
by Dan Close

Old bones grow cold.
I wish mine, then,
To have some sun and air
A view of mountains
A sight of the sea
Reminders of the earth's great curve.

Above me, for a blanket, thick-wove wheat.
Some charcoal situated in my green-baulked house
        would make a welcome hearth -
Finally, a fruit tree of some kind nearby.
And make sure either I, or just the place itself
Aligns properly and prominently with one, thus two, of
        the great directions -
This is most important, and advantageous to
        a good deep dream sleep.
And again, then,
This kind of virtuous and loving care
Also aids the great awakening.

Oh, and put my arrows there.
And my bow,
And fishnet.
And my music.

after she died

by Mary Brancaccio

just a scrolled bed and an oxygen tank and the terrible emptiness of her house, now that she was not there to welcome me home, now that i could not throw my arms around her body and pull her into the self of me. i found her stacks of mail, sorted bills, ones she made me write out in her last weeks when she was too tired to do more than sign her name. how she would ask me to read a bill and wait a moment to summon up a thought, how she was irked by my brother's bill from the marina because he never paid for his own fuel for his boat but left it on her charge, but then she said, pay it anyway. how she worried my father drank too much, how she had made him put the tv in the basement so he couldn't pass the day watching fox news and sports and drinking bourbon, and it wasn't like he drank too much, but she was sure it wasn't good for him at all, and she wanted him to go on living. how she posed in the photo on the kitchen shelf, her chemo cap on, her loose clothes, her arms spread out before a giant white azalea in full bloom, the smile on her face pure joy, that day that dad drove her home after her weekly treatment and she spotted the bushes outside town hall and made him pull a u-turn just to go back and look. the camera was in the car from their last trip, and he captured her amazement, her love of beautiful things, the abundance of it all. and in the cupboards hoards of vitamins and pills and chinese herbs and other things to make her well that didn't. and in the fridge the morphine that never did enough in the end to stave off suffering, how she would arch off the bed in terrible pain and none of us knew, not even her, when it would come on and how long it would last. and my father dreaming of building her muscle back by propping her on a exercise bike, how desperately he wanted her well again, how he prayed for what would never come, how he broke down sobbing on the day I had to tell him that the doctors said, there's nothing left to try, it's over, it's time to think a different way about things, and how she wanted to be waked in the church which wasn't something we'd ever done but what country people did, and she liked the idea: how quiet and cool it was, with the soft sound of water in the baptismal font and the hushed carpet of the main church, the smell of beeswax candles and the click click click of ladies' high heels on the tiles in the alcove, how strange she looked at the wake in her wig and make-up, not at all like herself but enough to fool most people. but then i was left in the house with silence: i wanted something to fill it up but not flowers, the stench of lilies like the odor of sickness and decay -- too sweet and not salty enough to believe they're really alive. how her hands and belly were bruised by the constant pricks of needles, how she withstood it all, how she wanted to know just what would happen when she died, how she insisted i ask the doctors, and when they said, is that it, is that what she wants to know? she stared back with her black eyes, yes, that's what I want to know. I want to know how I am going to die. months before she called me once on the telephone to tell me that she finally knew what was going to kill her: cancer, she just didn't know when, and that was some relief from the years of worrying about the wrong thing, and what if she loved me, what if she loved me more than i knew, and later, when i walked out of the church in spain and saw a massive gardenia filled with white blossoms and impossible incense i knew she wasn’t dead but she was somewhere far from me, and once in a while, i’ll smell those gardenias and think of how far she came, how much i loved her, how hard she was to love sometimes

Mausoleum
by Candace R. Curran

All the things I didn't say
came dredged from heavy stone
breathing with its own iron lung

I love you   *IN*   I love you   *OUT*

He knows

The one sided banter with the coffin
keeps a vigil for a safehouse
a place to rest remorse   a mausoleum
for forgiveness born again every day

I pray like a mime   a white faced fool
I'm listening for a pulse   a sign   music
from a porcelain doll

Can you hear me?   *IN*   Do you?

You could make a different world
from your dumb grave

Circle of Tears
by Charlotte Eulette

Know what our crying does?
It’s all the tears we’ve ever shed
that evaporates up
cloud level
and comes back down
to soak us
again, and again, again,
and then again.

Tides
by Victoria Field

The wind has scribed the sand
with unknown names in tongues
I'll never hear nor understand.
Rivers flow wine-dark along my naked legs,
between womb and sea, the hinterland.

Love fails again, what good
a passion spent? To cost so much
and still be insufficient?

The turning tide will erase the day.
No sea defence can keep the years at bay.
There was nothing there
and nothing here again today -
just a cradle for the empty air,
the space between my arms and hair.

Father

by Victoria Field

—from a line by George Szirtes

My father carries me across a field.
How did you enter this field?
Foxily, through a hole in the hedge
under cover of darkness and birds' nests.

My father carries me across a field.
What sort of field?
Tussocky, chaotic with cows,
desire lines leading through brambles and gorse.

My father carries me across a field.
Are you too tired to walk?
I'm just a child who might go astray.
His strong arms hold me close to his heart.

My father carries me across a field.
Is he a farmer, your father?
No, he loves black earth, broad beans,
horses and beer, but the land isn't his.

My father carries me across a field.
And then?
He's opened a heavy gate and gone through
disappeared down a deep lane among trees.

There's no one carrying me across a field,
just a tweed cap, flat in my hands
holding thoughts of winter days
and a faraway voice, calling the way.

Was it for this you were Born?
by Chiaboh Fidelis Fumbui

Was it for this you were born?
To embrace death before getting old?

And you lie here waiting to be buried.
And your parents sit there with long faces.

Is this why you were sent to school?
To acquire certificates that will end in toilets?

We waited for you to return in a limousine
But you returned in this casket.

Is this how selfish you were?
To bring a car no one can share with you?

I do not think you were born for this.
Go, go, go and take death along with you.

For we will stay a little longer
And take care of those you abandoned.

Poetic Madness
by Sharon A. Harmon

—from a mother whose child has died

She carved her world out of words—
at least when she wasn't busy carving
her delicate wrists. Pictured herself
as Savannah from *The Prince of Tides,*
Sylvia Plath, and on optimistic days
even fantasized about Emily Dickinson,
thoughts pouring from her pen.
She groped amongst her fears and dreams,
spent many nights in her moonlit garden,
spent tangled days in knotted sheets,
in twilight hours, in drug-induced sleep.
She drove to beaches to interview pebbles
and waves and sunsets, to find new
meaning, any meaning, to find cause to tell,
to genuinely forget about the other hell.
She saw words in trees, in clouds,
in sunbeams, moonbeams. The words
wove worlds and the words spewed forth words
because when all was said and done
In the Beginning, There was the Word, and after all
She carved her world out of words…

The Grief Mobile
by Sharon A. Harmon

clutching the wheel
tears streaming
down my face

landscapes flashing by
sun glinting on lakes
familiar old landmarks
to remind me,
songs on the radio
that sinks straight to my heart

I box my grieving between
these metal walls
find the solitude of
longing for you overwhelming

I don't care who sees me
although usually, no one does,
moving from mile
to mile with my memories,

thinking how swiftly time can go
I picture myself
flying into
your arms again...

Hoy decidí no llorar

por Lisa "Rubi G." Ventura

—en memoria de Arturo L. Gil

Al principio no entendí
pensé que iba a colapsar
que no era capaz de soportar
tanta angustia, tanto dolor
pensé que ahogaba en agonía.

no quise sentir
no quise vivir
no quise pensar en la melancolía que existiría
en la soledad que me perseguiría día tras día
en el vacío que quedaría donde una vez vivías.

pero ya se me fue el temor
ya no siento más rencor
sí fue tu partida que me enseñó
sobre el amor intencional
sobre lo sanativo que es vivir y recordar.

de tu partida aprendí
a aceptar que por más feo
o bonito que sea el destino
fue justo así que nuestro Señor
lo quiso.

de tu partida aprendí
a luchar por mis sueños
a apreciar todos los momentos
a demostrar con pasión mis sentimientos
por si acaso el mañana decide no llegar.

solo por hoy
quiero imaginar que sigues a mi lado
que ahora eres nuestro resguardo familiar
que permaneces despierto si no te dejamos de hablar.

a veces creo sentir
tu presencia, tu calor
a veces creo escuchar
tu nombre, tu voz
es un recordatorio fenomenal.

fe en el todo poderoso me curo la infelicidad
me aseguró de que todo iba a estar bien
porque nos íbamos a volver a ver--
en mis sueños o en la eternidad donde te podré abrazar
contarte todo lo que ha surgido desde la última vez que
nos vimos.

tu partida nunca se me va a olvidar
y aunque derrame un mar de lagrimas
prometo que en vez de lamentar
te voy a celebrar.

por fin comprendo que la vida continúa
hay que reír, hay que gozar
hay que explorar y experimentar
para que las despedidas no hayan sido en vano.

aunque no estes
hoy intento ser feliz

intento orar por ti en mi sagrado altar
intento ofrecerte luz a cambio de paz

yo no sé mañana
pero hoy escojo celebrarte en vez de llorarte.

hasta luego, ángel guardián.

Comet
by Zeina Azzam

Comets "leave behind a dusty trail of rocks and ice that lingers in space long after they leave."—The New York Times

You once filled my night sky.
Now, through the trees at moonlight
I search for your green-gray eyes
in faraway ice crystals,
your white hair in the comet's tail.

And these rocks on my path
chipped with stars of mica and quartz—
were they left over from your journey
through the solar system?
Shards from constellations you helped create?

I keep looking for you in them, everywhere.
In your trail between planets and asteroids,
the opaque cumulus clouds on a bright day.

Then at night I climb Orion's Belt,
travel below the horizon to the southern sky
and back.

I wake and remember
that you escaped into incandescence.
My memories have become your last breath,
rocks, ice, stardust.

All Souls
by Susan Marsh

Awakened at the wolf hour
Wanting near the ones so dear
The ones we say have passed
As if they had floated upward
And away to somewhere
We can't see or follow.

Even places have passed on;
I longed last night for one
longed for that lost place
my lost husband and all the souls
who have opened and passed
through the door of the past.

The wolf hour now has passed.
I dreamed I shared company
with a man I did not know
but who reminded me of you.
We sat on the top rail
of a corral, watching the horses.

He wrapped one heavy
wool-clad arm around me
long enough to offer friendship
before we parted ways. He took
the pain out of my yearning,
And for that moment

Life and death and earth and sky
once again formed a circle
that included me.

this sheaf of wind
by Suzanne S. Rancourt

levels itself against port city
plains – cutting wheat & oats
carving earth around
olive trees spiral
young almond trees with fruit
still covered soft bristles in green
unsuspecting lightness

no crack between night & day
sharp whistles morning birds echo
down narrow walking streets
bounce side to side begging
for ears their own brand of auricle
when sleep doesn't come
when nothing leaves without arrival
when there are no departed

Molting
by Yehudit Silverman

Where I sit
nothing is familiar

A Cooper's hawk
lands too close
red eyes search for prey
black beak
ready to crush
pretty little birds
dancing in air

Instead
she looks at me
the newly orphaned

Is the scent of sadness that strong?

As if on cue
this predator prances
three steps forward
three steps back
a ritual
of meeting?
of mourning?

I do the same
my body becomes bird
bird becomes beauty
beauty becomes beating heart

Rain
in this late afternoon light
once an aria of sweetness

Now
in this landscape of grief
muted with memory

My mom
wore a red velvet hat
with a blue feather

after she took her last breath
we put it on her head

The fashion of farewell

My dad wore nothing
at the end
just his mind
clear
circling
like a hawk

No one told me
even my skin would ache with longing
that this gold wedding band
my mother wore for 75 years
would now be mine

That nothing would ever be the same

that predators could become dancers
that before pretty birds disappear
I would molt
shed the feathers of who
I once was
and stand alone
shivering

Yield

by Dorinda Wegener

In the river, sledges of ice
off the dried banks. The last
corn has been cut; the field, felled.
These are harvest givens:
stubble will rot and go to post;
rime will thicken on beds,
culled crop; now not, my house—
a photo box of stills;
hidden in pantry, preserve jars
aborted; minutes embalmed in hours.
What grows the length of a nail
harrows the rooted vetch. My season
corollary: sod, a coulter
blade, six pome seeds. Should not
a mother search for her lost
share; would not the scion
surrender?

Good Grief
by Roger West

If Hope is the thing with feathers,
Then Grief is the thing with teeth and with claws.
That thing that sits on your sideboard,
Red-eyed and ragged and raw,

There among photos and keepsakes
Of the one you are keeping close to your heart.
It snarls when you enter the room
And swipes at you each time you pass.

But it really can't help being like that.
Like all savage beasts it's not readily tamed.
Accept it and know, as you get on with your life,
Given time, it will do the same.

It will still howl, it will still growl.
But you'll both learn how to rub along together
Show it some love and compassion;
And yes, it might even grow feathers.

So let it sit up there on your sideboard,
Don't hide it away, lock it up in a drawer.
For without Grief there is only oblivion.

Without Grief there can be no before.

Journeying

The Third Night
by Judith Yarnall

No need to hurry. No need to sparkle. No need to be anyone but oneself. Virginia Woolf's words—written in a confident hand on a small chalk board above the radiator on the way into your kitchen, where you and your children would pass them several times a day. Your hand always steadier than mine, a hand for calligraphy and fine-tipped camel's hair brushes. When you were fourteen I paid you to design a placard for William Blake's words, *Energy is Eternal Delight.*

Now there are no words, no desires. They haven't been pummeled out of my skin; paralyzed rather by the police tape stretching across the future: *Do not enter. Nothing beyond makes sense.* I used to have a desire so strong and natural that I had no need to recognize it—a desire not to outlive my children. Now the endlessly accumulating present presses in and no one comes closer. You are gone.

I think of Woolf with her pockets full of stones, walking towards the cold beckoning river. It is March 1941, seven months into the Blitz, four months after my birth. Hard to believe, but that may have been a time worse than ours, Kate. Bombs again like swollen rain but not falling this time on us. Cold water, cold stones, pebbles on the beach by our house. Lake rocks, pretty zebra ones of quartz and slate, one now marking the grave of my last cat Miep. And ragged ones, the petrified mud that you preferred because you found fossils within. Drop them with force and there they were: shell prints small as a baby's thumbnail. Remnants of the Champlain Sea. No police tape barring the past.

You are ashes, your memory, your work an ember illuminating many. And now? The Hebrew words do not lie naturally on my tongue. I hold the shamash, bend toward the slim candles and all but one go out.

There are no words—you hadn't had them for days before your death. There is only light.

Molly
by Rodger Martin

As sea waves of grief wash over the sand, know
this a necessary acknowledgment of loss.
Know, each recession of cleansing, salty liquid
erodes a grain or two of pain. Know her spirit
footloose and free of limit, again splashes
along the beachy shore of an ocean. Know
she gifts these tears, these memories:
Preparations for the heart to blossom again. Know.

Let her eat cake
by Amanda Shedonist
— *A poem for Kala Joy*

I stand at the sink washing dishes
No matter what else has happened
so must the dishes
In this case the dishes are a sidenote of joy
against a backdrop of melancholy
The news filtered in this afternoon
Social media lit up with remembrances
with photos and woe
A dear sister had passed
after dancing with death for years
Death finally dipped her too far
But before that...long before that
she had looked it right in the eye
She had not wanted to wage chemical warfare
within her own body
so she tried to make her body an inhospitable place
by waging war on her own demons
making peace with her anger
removing her fear
so there was nothing dark for it to cling to
She journeyed to the dark places within
and came back with poetry
She reflected on her words as her children
when in life her womb bore none
She let them take it to slow the sickness
Still she birthed more words
more creative and inspired than before
Her struggle to keep food down
led to poems of past food remembered

In one poem she prays...
"to the sky, the moon, the stars,
oh surely the stars will hear her wish
And grant it as the crickets dressed in powdered wigs
And french corsets laced tight sing her refrain.
Let her eat cake.
Let her eat cake.
Let her eat
CAKE!"
I had long since left social media
and had been sitting with my memories and her poetry
when I read this stanza
So I made a cake to honor her memory
and her lust for life
It made dirty dishes
but they are a sidenote of joy
for there will be cake
and I will eat it for her

N.B. This poem contains an excerpt from "Thin Woman" by Michelle Neve, reused with permission.

Every Heart a Door
by KB Ballentine

Owl ghosting the woods,
  you came back from the dead.

The weight of your words
  shadows me into midnight's

shocked silence,
  only the whisper of wings

floats through winter's stillness.
  How could love not

be enough for Time
  to re-design just one of us?

Falling snow feathers my skin,
  each crystalline star a miracle.

And I really do believe you are here.

Friend
by Wallace Fong

You do not always know how I feel,
but I'm glad you came. How I needed
this fellowship of silence between
few good words. The world I once
knew in is now a stranger to me,
and what expedient love there was,
there is none left. So, I'm glad that
you came to sit a while with me,
though when I say "you", it could
also be me.

What I might Say To Death

by D. Dina Friedman

Please, just one more cup of tea.
Will it be cold? Will there be latkes?
What should I tell the children

when they're making the latkes?
Will I be able to see
where you're taking me?

Some perch on a cloud,
or a blurry land of souls. Can I be
a hungry ghost chatting up the newbies?

Who are you, exactly?
A whirlpool? A fiery tree?
Do you smile? Do you wear sunglasses?

Will I need sunglasses?
Do I have to leave my stuff?
Can I be buried with a latke pan?

My poems? An onion?
Can I listen to music?
My music. Not harps.

How can I kiss the children
without upsetting the latke pan?

For A Survivor Who Sits With Death
by Felicia Mitchell

There has to be a reason
tucked inside this gift,
something you can unwrap
the way we unwrap bandages
and see scars
(scars that prove we are alive).
But death is not as easy as that,
not half as easy
as scars we carry on our skin.
These scars sear the soul
and heal over—sometimes red,
sometimes clean as surgery.
They do not fade.
They never whisper,
"This is the reason for the season."
We just have to guess.

Maybe grief is a babushka doll
God wraps in death and hands to us
to remind us to keep peeling back the layers.
No matter how many times
you lift a face from a nest of faces,
another face appears,
until your loved-and-lost one
gets smaller and smaller, the size of matter,
yet is always there,
always whole and holy,
powerful in his infinitude, or hers,
or his and hers or his and hers and theirs,

and all God's creatures too,
everything that lives and dies
and shrouds itself in something
finer than linen—a mystery, a gift,
a grief that never lets us finish opening it.
This has to teach us something.

My Father Could Take Apart a Dryer
by Jefferson Navicky

He said to my mother: you're the only one who can
handle me,
which meant: I'm a motherfucker and I love you.

I'm tempted to say, the ear doesn't do enough work in
fatherhood.

My father listens to birds feeding,
emphasis on waiting, clink of breakfast
spoons on a morning porch, my mother
after fifty-two years of eating together.
He's trying to teach me something
about losing him, but I can't hear it.

Inside the sound is the name
for the ability to take apart a dryer,
making sure the power's in the right place,
disconnected, then connected.

I will bring you the flowers
by Tommy Twilite

my slippers are a loaf of bread
my bed is a burrito
my eyes are two black olives
and my head is a block of cheese
you don't believe me
well it's true
I can see what you are too
you are the heavy dew
on a fall morning
you are brightly colored leaves
that turn brown
wandering like a fawn
in the meadow
you are a sparrow
I am just waiting for the sound
of your birdcall
to bring me down
my soul is a washing machine
my spirit an electric oven
my fingers are a glass of wine
red wine like blood
and everything I am
is made of love for you
you are something like the tall grass
that dances in the wind
you are moving like the waves
and the scent of your being
brings me closer to the moon
I know what you are doing

and it is driving me nuts
so don't forsake my plea
I will be your sidewalk
I will be the cinder block foundation
under your house
I will be your pickup truck
your hammer and nail
your oil change
your vacuum cleaner
I will be your underwear drawer
your sweet smelling soap
I will be clean towels dried on the clothesline
of your sunshine
if you will just be my queen bee
I will bring you the flowers

Speak, Memory
by Geri Gale

Speak, memory
of lavender
the taste
of a ruined peach
Speak, memory
for memory's sake
hurried breath
memory speak
memory repeat.

Memory speaks
something stored
something lost
merry marry memory
merrily marrying
a lost memory.

Speak, memory, speak
hungry for visitations
desperate for undeath.

Trappings
by Dorinda Wegener

The night sky passes to a paler shade.
The lake ice has gone out, dredging

the morning fog through the patch garden.
At the east window, what have I built?

Bone cradle, stolen blood, what shelter
with occupants, miniature and contained:

Lionels without track;
a doll with one eye; time-dried

boxes of rookies, reeds, and lace;
glass shooters. The rafters are full

of ghosts: the bassinet in the far corner
is seen, even now, lambent, through

the mote haze: wooly bear, fresh buntings
the flesh, buttercream. Now the sky

has reached its high blue; at windowpane,
no plant yields fruit. I have dressed

again, this wooden berth. I swear
to you, I live alone.

Where My Father Resides
by Zeina Azzam

Remembering him
is like ruminating over
an open-ended question.
My thoughts undulate
in the memory of his white curls
then slide and dissipate
into airless
space.

I sense my father's passing
as a limitless event,
the path of a star
or the lines of a heartbeat
monitor, replicating and
moving forward
off the
screen.

When the dark indigo
vastness of night blankets me,
I lie awake thinking
of comets and galaxies,
infinite trajectories
where my father
now
resides.

Years: A Koan
by Subhaga Crystal Bacon

Nothing is last, nothing first.
Everything is a wheel. Here
and here and here with no room
for there. Even infinity loops
back on itself. While dark,
also bright. Up, also down. Try
to mark what ends from what starts.
Walk on this spinning ball east to west
or north to south, and the place you began
is also moving, like the horizon
out of reach.

Stand still and ride
through the night sky that holds
the morning light. Morning.
The crescent moon hangs
like a comma in the sentence
of your life. Follow it.

On a Morning like This

by Subhaga Crystal Bacon

The frozen silence seems to sing
in this bowl of white that sweeps
up and out toward sky. Not the wind
scouring down from snow, carrying
the northern light, scent of ice.
The ice itself is a music faintly glinting.
Trees, those lone sentinels, exclaim
along the ridge the song of wood
circling itself around a still heart
drinking deep from earth. And the river.
Moving its ever changing self
over rocks, flickering under frozen
eddies like a flame. Like the fire
popping in the grate, last summer's
rain in the cut grain of pine.

Webbings of Light
by KB Ballentine

Thursday laughed, tendrils of green waving
from all directions, redbuds meandering the woodline.

Spring erupts – grays and browns shimmering
into yellow and white, purple that leaps

from the mountains into the yards.
Pendulum noon skips past the clouds, the rain,

leaf-litter quilting the forest floor.
Finches peep from the hedgerow.

The dead rising, blushed with promise –
singing.

Come Spring
by Anne Bergeron

A flock of pine grosbeaks
chose to winter nearby

their whistles lilt like flutes
in thickets of tall white spruce

they call   and I   (still here)
look up   at steely sky

not down   at shifting ground   where
your footprints in snow are not.

You'd love how rose-bellied males
chirp rejoicings at the feeder

their expectations so easily met
as I scatter fistfuls of oily black seeds

how late-day light gilds
each lift and turn of black-striped wing

how they sing as they settle in to roost
as you hummed and read to me before sleep.

No one has asked   (but I will tell you)
here's what I miss the most:

it's not only how you'd leap and run
to take my hands in yours

but how that august day   you knelt
beneath a maple's mottled shade

touched lobelia's blue-starred tips
caressed the curving calyx   delicate as dew

whispered to yourself   (and me)
whatever it is you want   don't wait.

This long winter   wants the open doors of spring
but snow piles up on porch and roof

and there's only one way
out of the house.

But when I can think
I think of you

because buds will swell
even though you're gone

and your smile still brings
warm   warm rain.

The Seasons of Life: A Poem for Julia
by E.M. Burton-Crow

The seasons of life are like a
journal whereupon our stories
are written on color-tinted pages,
Beginning with the green,
fecund shades of Spring,
Then glowing big and bright and
yellow in the Summer sun.

Too soon the winds of Autumn
turn those pages orange and brown,
Like the falling leaves and dusty
wheat fields who've just
relinquished their bounty.

Then one crisp morning, frost
descends, slowing down the
water enough that we can
finally, truly appreciate her beauty,
Glistening crystals humming
with a song tuned by billions of
previous Winters.

Grey, white, silver pages.

Plus when the light hits just
right, The full spectrum!

Releasing rainbows who before
now remained hidden inside
each Unassuming drop of water.

The same molecules that
comprise most of our matter.

And most of what matters…

Though in this life we are
promised but one journal, at
least it is a spectacular one,
Its many pages bursting with
hues beyond our
comprehension.

No one can know for sure what
book comes next, but above all
else the Nature of the Seasons
shows us:
Time—like all things in the
Universe—is but a cycle,
Each ending a new beginning,
And each beginning a new ending.

Opposites meeting again as old
friends, enriched by the wisdom
gleaned with each passage.

I Loved the Laughter
by Dan Close

I loved the laughter of my father's folk,
Attained through years of toil and grime.
The winning satisfaction of a well-turned joke
Or of a rude description, just well-timed.
For they were rough-hewn peasants, they themselves
Were sired by an Irishman who crossed the seas
And settled in a coal patch in the hills
Of eastern Pennsylvan-i-ay. I'd hear
Them jibe and laugh when work was done;
I'd see them sit around the bar.
Six sons they were and they knew how to laugh
And what to laugh at; sure of that –
The fact of simply making it another day,
Still with their lungs filled with the smear of coal.
Because of that, their getting old was redefined.
Born old and cold and getting better as they aged,
For somehow things got better through the years.
Behind their laughing eyes you still could see
The deprivation and the strife. They passed all that
And all their laughter at it down to me.

When Friends Die
by Charlotte Eulette

He didn't expire or pass away—
he died.
We didn't "lose" him either.
You can say it—"died."
All that he was
while here on this land
goes with him, and with him too
the hardihood of friendship.

Often, we think and feel
that when friends die,
they linger here awhile,
to walk along the streets of our city,
the ones paved with desire;
to walk through the woods;
walk with dogs the way we used to;
walk in the park past the rose garden
and sit at our shady bench;
walk lakeside by the fountain
and watch it fountain together;
and back down to the lake,
around the museum and auditorium
and past the closed Vienna hotdog stand, still there.

When my friend died
he had so many experiences
and bold times
shared with me and you
that got gathered in his *life-on-Earth bundle.*
Like a hobo carrying
a stick with a bundle tied on the end.
We go *with him.*

He will unpack us and we'll rove.
He knows we'll materialize
and animate the love made, that's always.

He died, we live, we'll die and they'll live.
All of our friends gather about, back-and-forth.
We flow naturally.
Smothered with love. It's all we are to know.

Tranquilo
by Charlotte Eulette

—In Spanish, the word "tranquilo" is sometimes offered to help people calm down, or take a breath.

The beachcomber dogs digging holes
to bury the setting sun each night
in the Pacific Ocean.
Tranquilo, tranquilo.

The old lady in the church
touches your dim trembling hand
with hers, crevassed.
To soothe only you.
The lentil *sopa* boils over the stove
wafting spice and garlic.
The man in the wheelchair who lost his legs
asks for help via a paper coffee cup.
The man who lost his faith once long ago.
Maybe you will find it and return it to him some day.
My mother's pink sweater I wore for many days
while tending to her dying
—her last breath—
she, for my first breath—fair exchange.
Tranquilo.

The lavender scarf in the wind
flying under the bridge anywhere.
Her gold tooth glows
in the night's fluorescence
as she smiles making wild tortillas.
The Hairdresser rinses your hair
thinking about her young daughter her mother
is watching. No men in the family anymore.

Uncle Gus by the grave puts some money and cigarettes
out beneath the wreath
so workers don't take
the frozen funeral flowers away yet…*Just another day please.*
The ducks and geese and seagulls
getting along so well
on Chicago's Lake Michigan city shore.
The crows politely wait in the distance
for their turn to be nearer.
Tranquilo, tranquilo, tranquilo.

Cousin Niki and her pounced-on heart.
Much love brewing all the time.
Tranquilo.

Her sister, cousin Dina's sharp mind asleep now.
Tranquilo.

Love/Joy arena in our Souls.
Love Tokens spent.
We have only so many—can't replenish
and oh so valuable—when you give them out.
You know it so—each of you—
way down deep in the hush we share.
With hands pressed together,
make aloud your
Tranquilo.

After I Die…

by Chiaboh Fidelis Fumbui

After I die and can no longer speak,
let the evil words I planted whither
but let the good, like a fig tree, sprout.

After I die and can no longer see,
let the evil I saw be forgotten
but, like a smile, let clean drops show.

After I die and can no longer erect,
let the heartbreaks be forgotten
but, like the sun, show my kids love.

After I die and can no longer sweep,
let the dirt under my bed be burnt
but let the words of hope I wrote be read.

After I die and can no longer hunt,
forgive me for the animals I killed
and thank God for the ones spared.

After I die and can no longer fell trees,
don't fell any more for my casket.
Let me feel the embrace of mother earth.

After I die and leave this space free
let whoever occupy it, do so well
and give these plants a chance to grow.

Whether you saw me weak or brave,
where my head lies in my grave,
plant, for the world, a fruit tree
that will, in the wind, dance free.

After I die, you are free to judge me
but be fair on a man who can't speak.

Still, You Must Sing
by Wallace Fong

The day will come
when you will be lifted
out of the centre
into the margin
and the world which had
warmed to you
will remember you no more.
Thus will begin
your immense loneliness.
You will talk only to yourself,
you will sing like a sparrow
on empty branches.
Still, you must sing,

Lines for My Tombstone

by Georgia Gojmerac-Leiner

I lived in the earth, in the flowers,
In the vegetables, in the worms, in the weeds,
In the rain, in the sunlight,
In the fold of my family.
In poems.
A wordsmith,
I once soothed the sick and dying;
I did my small part
On the planet.

If You Supposed Heaven
by Georgia Gojmerac-Leiner

If you would extract
from the summer,
a high life,
then you would plan a garden
seasons ahead.
Phlox my mother gave me
before she dreamed of dying,
has grown into a small forest
of purple, lavender and pink,
colors that no crayons come in.
Butterflies have been my company,
my mother would have known the joy
of this feeling of being born again.

And if you would have a party of senses,
eyes, ears, nose, mouth and skin,
you would sit on your farmer's porch
with a mix of memories and excitement,
and you would burrow vicariously
with the butterflies, bees and humming birds
into the micro vials of flowerets
with the pointiest part of your
face imaginable,
and pose for pictures with
the creatures of translucent wings,
the piloting dragonflies.

If you had such a garden
on which you would get high
on the nectars of life,
you would not want to merely live by it
but be it.

And if you supposed you were in heaven,
your supposition would be true.

Luck Instructions

by Betsy Guttmacher

float in the eye of a kettle pond
surrounded by a circle of foliage
white cedar, red maple and pitch pine
suspend yourself in leafy silence
ears below the water line

you are a plastic fork
your family are napkins
your friends are pie plates
we are a picnic

later something will grow over the spot
where the blankets and snacks lie
maybe another thing will dig up
your fossilized grapes and wonder

about the butter and honey sandwich
for the one that doesn't like ham
but will be starving by midafternoon

Veronika en juin
par Amy Suzanne Heneveld

Un soir d'été en juin,
la lumière s'éteint,
des rires, du chant,
une fête d'anniversaire.

Nous avons amené des cadeaux.
Assis en cercle près d'un arbre,
on a parlé, en mangeant des fraises,
en buvant du champagne.

L'arbre sous lequel nous étions assis
poussait du sol dans le crépuscule.

Nous avons dansé dans la pataugeoire
toi et moi.
L'eau peu profonde, d'un bleu électrique, où des
points de lumière
se reflétaient, cette nuit éternelle.

Je suis passée par cette pataugeoire
l'autre soir, la nuit tombante et tu étais là,
clapotant, chantant, jouant,
ton trente-et-unième anniversaire.

L'année d'après tu aurais eu trente-deux.

Maintenant tu deviens vielle avec moi.
Je t'imagine dans les yeux
des enfants que je vois,
dans les miens peut-être,
dans les visages ronds des femmes
d'Europe de l'est

aux corps puissants et aux yeux clairs,
aux gestes nerveux.

J'aurais voulu te connaitre
toutes nos vies. J'imaginerai
que c'est ainsi, où peut-être
c'est là le problème, une vie
ne peut jamais nous appartenir.

Veronika aimait lire des histoires
du New Yorker et des romans
en anglais par John Updike.

Elle aimait le faire sur la plage.
Une photo d'elle nue sur un hamac
en train de lire, au soleil.

Keepers
by Joan Hofmann

Like my mother now passed, I wash out plastic bags
to use again. Pint-sized, sandwich, quart.
Plastic containers from the deli, take-out. I rinse out
glass jars from mayonnaise and jelly. I stack
newspapers for box stuffing, wood-stove starting.
I fold wrapping paper, slowly removing tape.
Ribbon, bows, gift bags, peanut packing. I hold onto
his daring looks, her smiles of support. Sunlight on
the wavy-glass windows, darting hummers at
the feeder, seeds from last year's Sweet William,
geranium stalks in cold storage, begonia branches
over winter. I massaged my mother's legs, propped
my father's head. I hold a blanket he used, wear her
sweater still.
Peaches, magnolia leaves scattered on the lawn.

I plant the pansies they loved,
all around me.

The Kids Keep Asking Me About Death

by Linea Jantz

I know what the rain means
It means the river is coming home
from the ocean

I still miss you
on a random Friday in November
droplets chirping on the water like tiny frogs

The kids keep asking me about Death
I say everyone dies
eventually

Will I die?
Hopefully not for a long time

A lone seagull swoops the currents
above a river crisscrossed in mallards
I cry in the dark

Beaver float the channel
I see marks of teeth on the willows.

Bees Dance
by Earl Livings

And no one died that day,
not ever, they flew out
their bodies like bees
from a flower taking nectar
to the hive, honeycomb light
sweetening the next day
and the next, till the season
turns grey, as it must…

Yet, light always summons
shoot, bud, blossom,
the bees sounding out
their dancing paths
again and again,
hives busy and lush,
stamen dust flung far,
wildflowers brightening forests,
and a man spoons honey
into a cup the day after
his friend suddenly slipped
out of his body

The Future Melts

by Janet MacFadyen

You could hold it in your mouth
like chocolate.
What comes of this is desire, and if you taste it
what comes is plenty, it is so sweet.
Then what comes
is that point of stillness inside the body.
That is why cats are so liquid.
That is why the leaf
floats down and down in the warm air though it is fall,
and thoughts slow like a train
coming to a halt in the middle of a cornfield,
at night, in October, with starlight shining down.
You could get off here in the darkness with the others
quietly talking and looking up at the stars,
whose light has traveled from so far away
and so long ago.

Revelation at Philpott Lake
by Felicia Mitchell

I don’t think the soul leaves the body;
it has to be the other way around,
the way a berry leaves its bramble
or a bird leaves its nest.
It has to feel a little like I feel
after I swim and I leave the water,
my arms leaving a whole lake behind.
What if the body leaves the soul
to give the soul more room to wander?
What if the soul is thankful,
hovering, a dragonfly over water?

Everything Belongs
by Robert Eugene Perry

I am a tree, grown up
twisted and gnarled from
bending backwards towards
the light, having spent
too much time
in shadow.

I am a stream, flowing
hither and yon, picking up
stuff meandering through
strange lands, sometimes singing
often murmuring seeking
an ocean.

I am a cloud, pursuing the heights
blown about and set off course
filled with moisture and vapors
stretched out and dissipated
at times reflecting the colors
of the sun.

I am the Universe, born of stardust
a miracle of contradictions
energy and matter, moving and static
constantly changing and adapting
neither created nor destroyed, only
Being.

October Ghosts
by Robert Eugene Perry

In October my ghosts don't wait for Hallows Eve
They come early to check out this year's foliage
To talk of times that were, reinterpreting memories
As we walk through the forest, each moment
A grace I could not see while they were alive
They tell me nothing is ever wasted, ever lost
Pay attention to the way things come back to you
Spend yourself extravagantly, like these trees
Let everything go and you will discover
You have had everything you needed all along.

solid meander
by Katherine Pierpoint

—*i.m. Dave*

A pattern gets printed; in strings of loops,
as a habit of shine, in these reedbeds, or a scribble in air

Snaky mud-rivers under big, big skies
where waterlife is everywhere; half-seen but constant.
Place as fabric, as an endlessness, turning.

Now I want a coracle — and
that skinny, stand-up courage which coracles bring,
to go poling around in a trembly circle.
That Bronze-Age nerve.

Dark hollowed-out tree-trunks. Making fissured ways
over wetlands
to new god-creatures. Those stories
thrive in us utterly here — beyond time.
Holy fools. Us, our Beloveds. Earth's vast rivers of gold.

Great fistfuls of weather. Shouts in the skies, and
mad feather-heads topping old ditches.
Pug-marks. Reed-bed-rustle,
a papery, drypoint, scrawling sound. Of flames.

What do flames do? Rise, and jostle,
they fly to leave the fire, while still creating it;
my heart —what can they want?
they already *know* the rising.
The pure fire you can rest the gaze on,
rest the heart in a livingness,
for each flame moves freely all the time leaving the planet
while keeping its magnetised foot right there in the heart.

It's love's work made easy for us. Exciting, relaxing.
Yes, both. Love, the curve that bends   to meet, and meet.

Everything is paisley out here in the mudflats, the
marshes. Curling, uncurling …

Did the sky know us? when we walked its light edge?
Because the earth knew our dailyness—
the galley kitchen, our tree; the cats.
We held hands there often   on earth
our shared horizon went hazy
Is it the same sky, like a river?

Blue-white water through mud, shell, and bone. Solid
meander   looping, looping,
coming back to the point. The real point is,

I loved *all your shirts.* Our days.
Paisley prints — each vortex made safe,
each spiral a miniature drop of curving water.
Nutshell. Worlds

flex like echoes,   moving   moving through   now.
The smalted- or fig-blue cottons you liked to wear,
the lunar silver prints on royal-purple ground,
or those warm animal-browns, each tipped with gold,
like wild hair.
Mandarin collars. Coconut buttons; slightly warm,
slightly worn.
A faint, clean smell.
Bread   and fresh smoke   maybe salt.

Quiet café-table hands, Tuesday-afternoon-ish
synth-fade, the snake-coil slide of cables, and laying
down the music…   the point is,
one does already know one another   anywhere.
We found.

If anyone asked what you liked —
what was it, you liked best?
you'd answer, quite simply

'I like laughing' you'd say; then, quietly,
'Life as a dance, not a race',

joyous   your genius, calm   So natural,

so present.   Gone.

What She Saved
by Elaine Reardon

It is said when they opened her
first they found a snowstorm
from December 14, 1946,
when she married John in the Sacred
Heart Church. There was the feather
from her hat, a high-heeled pump,
an old corsage and menu
from their honeymoon in New York.

Further down there were bits of flannel,
lace, a small sewing machine that
whirred, making new clothes
from someone's bigger ones,
stitching nightgowns cut from worn
sheets, tiny shirts from bigger ones.

There were walking shoes,
a baby carriage that held
two of us when the walk was too long.
Tucked away were squares of fudge that sold
for two cents at the Jewish bakery we passed,
tattered recipes, oatmeal, walnuts,
fresh squeezed oranges, a sack of flour set
on a kitchen table, and our old stove heating up.
There was a radio on, maybe Count Basie playing,
or Tony Bennett crooning from the top of the
refrigerator.

Last, there were purple lilacs that grew at the front door,
and roses from the front garden that John grew for her.

Gilfeathers Turnips
by Elaine Reardon

*—For Carl, who shared his Gilfeather turnip seeds and joy
with all his neighbors*

They bought the old homestead
on Flower Hill Road,
cleared and planted the back meadow.
Now he could see north to green Vermont hills

On Flower Hill Road
he saved seeds
where he could see north to green Vermont hills.
Gilfeather turnips his favorite,

He shared Gilfeather seeds with neighbors,
said they were earthy and sweet.
Gilfeather turnips his favorite,
pulled after frost,saved in the root cellar,

buttery and fragrant right from the garden.
He planted in the cleared back meadow
to bring sweetness to winter.
They bought the old homestead.

To Irene on the Anniversary of Her Death
by M. Anne Sweet
—for Irene Drennan

We drink her funeral beer
blood wine
stingers of bees
her pierced body broken

Dying, she leaves us her wounds
her flesh raw
her savory   her sweet
her apple allegories
sashimi
pastries
the tree-grown orange
vinegar's bitter bite

At Any Time
by Steve Trombulak

He was riding in the car with his wife
After a day of skiing
Ice blue skies and a rush of wind
Among his final memories
Before the vessel burst
And he was gone long before
She pulled up in terror to the door
Of the emergency room

She was struck by a car
Whose driver trusted
Too much to his luck
Just as hers ran out
At the right intersection
But the wrong time
Just five minutes from home
And its hearth embrace

He had just finished playing
With his bandmates, *the Avant Guard Dogs,*
In his basement their rehearsal both tight and loose
In a way that only musicians
Who have played together for years can feel
He turned to one and said, "Man, it is so much fun to play with you"
And going upstairs to the kitchen
Collapsed without a good-bye

My mentor's note to me said
"The cancer is back and my time is done,"
But it was sent by his wife

After he'd already entered hospice
and into his final dreams

Her heart simply had had enough
And she slipped away at night
And he had had enough
Of a life compressed by depression
And he slipped away in the dark
And so it goes
And has gone
And will go on still

I do not write these words in rage
About the unfairness of life
But to remind myself of the
Ever-present imminence of death
We act as if the next hello is a given
Yet at any time in any moment
I could be gone
Good-bye is always implied

Because of what can be at any time
At every time I create what could be
Your last memory of me
Because of what can be at any time
At every time what I don't say
Could always be left unsaid
Because of what can be at any time
At every time what I do
Might never be undone

So to this I say
"Man, it is so much fun to play with you"
"What you wrote rocks my world"

"I hold so much gratitude for what you spoke today"
"I love what you do in the world"

Every time.

Wintering Over
by Rhett Watts

Hope rises in within the structure of things—
through the hollow rose canes left climbing trellis
and tips of maple limbs spreading open,
hands into the space around them.

Curls of Paper Birch rattle outside my window.
All over town exterior paint peels.
Last week's dirty snow flows in rivulets
down the street. Sand can bank there for months.

Paper Whites on my sill,
a gift from a friend, swell straight-stemmed
from cracked skins. Their clear scent lingers.

distance

by Joe Webster

you cannot have me there
i cannot have you here
but your beautiful words
span the distance
a bridge of breath
rhythm and rhyme
delicate as lilacs
strong as steel
i drink them with my soul
from a cup of longing
you are here
i am there

First Anniversary Prayers
by Carolyn A. Cushing

Dear Departed One,
The evening
became evening
became dark,
led you to Nowhere.

I knelt at that threshold
whispering all the words
I knew into Winter
night after long night
down on my knees.
I couldn't leave.

But Spring came and ice broke.
I mixed your ash in with the seeds
answered soil's call to be fed.
Prayers now in my palms,
under my nails, turning the earth.
I watched green take the field,
raise the vine, feed the bud
and blood of strawberry
opened my lips.

I walked then
in our old places
as green turned to flame,

turned to brown,
everything fell down
and this is the day
you’ve been gone
in all the seasons.

I’ve used up my prayers.

A white goose rises
so close I hear air lift each feather,
the sound of earth embracing sky,
turning me into the shift
where I no longer speak
but instead listen to hear
from the wind,
from the field,
from the snow
the prayer
you make now
for me.

N.B. The “evening became evening” is a line in W.S. Merwin’s Song for the Dead, a translation of a Romanian folk poem, from his Selected Translations (Copper Canyon Press, 2015).

Weekly Skype

by Earl Livings

—i.m. Wayne Francis Pinna (Reneé Horemans)

Obviously, we didn't know
this would be our last call,
the deepest and longest,
the first time we truly began
to know the brother
we both didn't know we had
till a bare dozen years ago.

'Cool,' you said in your way,
that hard, sharp 'C',
that 'oo' short and high-pitched,
with slight upward inflection.

You preferred sports to classwork,
yet after being told, 'We can't do much
for you here,' you knuckled down
at another school, because you could.
Then apprentice boilermaker,
though you ached to be a sparkie,
no choice because of the family,
but your choice to prove you were
more than the owner's son,
unbroken welding seams
better than others could do.

You raced speedway sedans,
guts, talent and trophies,
more guts in standing at the edge
of the infield as a photographer:
snap—sprintcar wheelies in mud,

snap—cars ramming and upending,
snap—that car screaming towards you,
running over your toes, your scowl turning
into a laugh and shoulder slap.
'Cool.'

We charted some of our twists
and turns of life, those byways
that could lead to regrets,
but not for you. Touched on
legacies, thanks, joys.

Giving the typical two thumbs up,
we signed off till next week,
your last 'Cool' echoing through…

After the Eulogy, the U L
by Diana Hirst

That's it. They've said goodbyes.
Some with real tears in their eyes,
some with a remembered joke.

Me? I'm free to spend Eternity
floating round this Library,
bent on after-life research.

First get my bearings, then explore
what is held on every floor
before deciding where to start.

Which disciplines attract me most?
What's easiest if you're a ghost?
What's the grounding that I lack?

Does it matter? I've got time.
All Eternity is mine
to weave my All-Embracing book.

N.B. The U L is the familiar name given to Cambridge University Library

Opening the Gate
by Victoria Field
—for D.K.

In five years, we had just two true conversations.
The first expansive, outside in sunshine, marriage

on both our minds – we were wedding guests
on a perfect May day, everyone joyful, dressed up

bubbling with mild hysteria. You acknowledged
a wistfulness, too, for those of us not, or not yet,

(and, now, never can be) - happily spliced.
At least that's what I read between your easy banter

and serious discussion of churches and religion – like me,
you seemed on the edge – half in half out

but yearning too, wanting to know more about
that one-way gate, the jeweled road tumbling towards

an amazing light and open arms. The second time
we talked one-to-one, was in winter, a cold, dead day

between Christmas and New Year. Kind friends
brightened the darkness with a party and games

but you, subdued, were not quite there -
told me it had been a dreadful year.

More and more, you said, you'd been in the cathedral
asking the questions it understands so well

but finding no answers. 'A permanent solution
to a temporary problem,' someone said, afterwards,

not seeing the solution's already a given –
the dilemma's not why, but how, what and when –

the why-nots of love, work and friends, irrelevant –
they'll all soon be gone, in any case. Not a moment of
madness -

you choreographed a small theatre of action – and then?
Was it a drop through cool dark to a nothingness of total
peace?

Or did you spiral skyward past blossom and birds
to the embrace of a bride, and the blue of her miraculous
eyes?

Our Animal Kin

Black, with One White Spot
by Earl Livings

I had never seen death throes before.
Watched your body roll upwards a moment
And stretch, as if you had suddenly awakened
From one of those nightmares you used to have.

Thought you would snap back to endearing ways:
Drinking from the bowl with your left paw.
Nuzzling my face with whiskers so I'd awake
And feed you—done only minutes before.

You hopped down, seemed to collapse
And stumble, as if a leg had given way,
Then, so swiftly I wasn't sure if in play or pain,
You crabbed and rolled across the floor

To settle without a sound on your right side,
One gurgle-cry as I stroked and checked
For broken bones, kept stroking, waiting
For that purr we would hear across rooms.

I had never buried a pet before:
A hole in the front garden you haunted daily.
Your fur-riddled blanket. The brush always welcomed.
Food for your journey through darkness.

A wind ruffles the roses on the grave.

Elegy for a Spring Squirrel
by Dan Close

Squirrel, I have not seen such courage in a long, long
time.
How you got to the side of Hollow Road I do not know.
Knocked out of a tree; sideswiped by a car –
The means of your death means nothing.
The manner of your death, everything.
You knew your death was coming.
You crawled to a place safe from the thundering cars.
You curled up in a circle of repose, your
paws against your chest,
your head tucked against
your breast.
No king in all of Christendom or out of it
Ever looked better on his bier,
And you did not need the accoutrements we use
To indicate your dignity.
You did it alone,
Alone with God and Universal Death.
Repose was in your soul,
waiting to come out.
It came. You went.
So may we all, with such sweet beauty.

Willow

by John Matthews

Your dear face
Looks back at me across the green.
I close my eyes to hold back tears.
Wherever I look I see you,
Your white fur soft as silk,
Your quiet song in my ears,
Your beautiful eyes.
Willow you were my friend,
My love, my true companion,
My teacher and my guide.
Now, almost beyond my touch,
You listen for my voice,
Waiting for the call
To walk again at my side,
Always one step ahead,
Looking back, checking
I have not lost the way.
But most of all I remember,
In these twilight days,
Waking to find you watching,
Great eyes regarding me,
Full of wisdom
Beyond anything I could know.
Simply, you are a cat,
Whiter than snow.
Subtly, you are much more,
More than words can capture.
I watch you now, in the sun,
One last warm moment

Before cold death reaches out.
My heart is yours always,
Dear one, soul queen,
Sweet princess of my life.
I will watch and wait
In these dark times
Until.... until.... until ....

Moon Review at the Emergency Vet
by Jefferson Navicky

I'm wearing the moon's white suit as I sit
beneath its hole, the clouds
a curtain for its one bald eye. A gurney

arrives, the sheet a curtain over
the night's first body.
A good white suit reflects duty

without a hint of dust that must,
I assume, accrue on the dead.
A miracle never happens

when I want it to. Whatever happens
seems to become a catastrophe I must
ask the moon to eat. This dark sea

of pavement under street light's glow
possesses sheen reflection logic.
Icarus knows what I'm talking about.

The television in the lobby quietly
plays a medical drama I can't
watch because a small being is dying

in the arms of a woman beneath
the TV. So I watch the moon
instead, its slow bit of advice

a masterpiece burned white hot

into my inner eye where I keep
tonight's tally of who won't make it,

who might. A slow-moving mosquito
goes in for the kill. Leftover
strawberry tops assert their blood

relations atop my white suit to
blood stains who show a stark refusal.
They leave me in a room to wait

where I can't see the moon. Slow jazz
played soft to keep me sane. It's lonely
in limbo. I check myself for light.

Love Song
by Linda Warren

All day our old grey cat walked in circles,
looking for a place to hide.
She was through with the world.

She'd been to the vet,
come home again with remedies,
but she was beyond the help of remedies,
beyond food or comfort, didn't want
the nest I made in the corner
or the pillow on the floor.

We let her wander.
She always liked to hide, liked laundry,
got into the drawer one time,
our underwear had fleas for months.

I couldn't watch her, went out to the garden,
dug up lilies, thought about things
older than the cat: marriage, kids, the shovel,
wrapped in tape where it cracked twenty years ago,
I don't remember who it was that broke it.

When I came in I found her curled up in the four inch
space
behind the desk, wedged between
the printer cable and the power cord.
You got the flashlight and the shovel,
And I brought her, wrapped in laundry.

Curled up the way she was, with her love of little places,
It didn't take a hole of great dimension,
And we didn't need to speak,
the number of holes we've dug, the two of us.

Where did we learn this choreography,
this dance essential to a marriage,
how to bury things?
And, having buried them,
walk back together to the house.

That First Walk After the Dog Dies
by Kathy Kremins

Shadows trail me as I autopilot down
the three times daily path we wandered

over eleven years, drowning in my head
snow crunching hard rock reverb

eyes recognize the light as it crystallizes
the Christmas holly, needing the object

to capture itself out of the dark surrounds
How we shined brightness on those crisp

cold, having-just-stormed walks
footpawprints indistinguishable

open to the gully of sky, swallowing
pine cones, leaf litter, bark shreds, meltings

I reach the river, trip, or is it a falling
from the disorientation of emptiness

hands dig deep into almost-flowering witch
hazel like sinking into curly amber neck fur

maintaining some balance while breaking
fleecy forest snow springs onto my face

a hundred wet nose kisses, my lost dog
wandering woods without my compass

Blues Hound
by Candace R. Curran

She stays in four days   five
doesn't bathe   doesn't do a little
this   a little that

She stays inside safe until
need turns her insides out where
she walks a ghostdog   staggering

back home to sleeping in
dirty sheets   crooked blankets
she can't straighten out

not now anyway   so she stays
'til a sunny day comes
and she can walk the dog's

remembrance   home again
drink and   eat something
face rooms filled with his

dog hair and shadows
the slowdance of sorrows in an
empty cradled   sway of limbs

Thank You
by D. Dina Friedman

for the sun filtering through the canopy of trees,
in the last of September's light. For the anticipation

of my grandchild's newborn hand, the happiness of
kicking feet.
Thank you for opening my heart

to questions, revealing
a path through the weeds to speak my truth.

Thank you for the authenticity of worms
under my calloused and encrusted feet. Thank you

for my old eyes, old thighs, for making
this October and November of my life blaze red,

before the leaves crumble; thank you for the wisdom
of those already crossed and those nearer to the gate,

for my grandmother's ghost hand on my shoulder
as I play the Moonlight Sonata on a cloudy night

urging me to squeeze harder on the melody. These notes.
They're the ones that matter, she always said. Thank you

for reminding me I matter, even as the landscape
turns to snow and still. For the nudge to remember

silver is the most beautiful color
even when tinged with gray, the blue

eventually breaks through. And when the sun casts
its rapturous light on a tree already ice-coated and dead,

when you have to place the cat's warm body in the
shallow hole
and rain the dirt on top of his fur. Remember

those nights with his nose in your neck, the way the
whiskers tickled you
into a tranquil state of doubtlessness that all was right
with the world.

Eileen's Cat Toots
by James Harpur

—After Christopher Smart
i.m. Toots (1986-2004)

I will praise Eileen's cat Toots
For she is chieftain of the pussy race
For she wears her tartan ribbon round her neck
For she bears the markings of a tortoise
For her snowy feet are soft as thistledown
For her cheeks are plump like pin-cushions
For her tail is a feather boa
For she concertinas out to be a draught excluder by the door
For she lies like the sphinx and folds her mits into her winter muffler
For her back leg is like a rabbit's and as bitable
For when she sees the movement of a sparrow she twitches forward,
every sense on red alert
For she is a wicked puss, an eater of God's creatures,
For she is a blessed puss, and knows not what she doeth
For when she leaps she stretches like a caterpillar and alights
as softly as a butterfly
For she tiptoes like a ballerina through the table's bric-a-brac
For she gets her artificial tan beneath the angle-poise
For her eyes are moss-green marbles of light
For her wee head fills her bowl of food when she crunches up
her fish-meal beans
For she eats her blobs of porridge from your finger
For she is a waif with a look of desolation when she cries out for more food
For her tongue laps the vase's water like a tiny darting goldfish
For her teeth are sleek and creamy like bone needles
For she biffs her mouse of silver foil and lays in ambush below the table
For she can't resist an interest in the drumming of the fingers
For on bonfire night she creeps two millimetres from the floor
For when it thunders she seeks her air-raid shelter in the washing basket
For when she arches up her back she is a Chinese bridge
For she looks so innocent when told she'd make a nice fur hat
For she settles on the window sill to greet you home from work

For she steams in from the cat flap: entry pursued by a Tom
For at night she is a furry-covered waterbottle at your feet
For when she wakes she lifts a sultry peeper and yawns out her claws
For she sits in backyard sunlight and lifts a drumstick leg to lick her fur
For she's a tiger in her jungle of lupins and gladioli
For she is a wee angel, agnus dei, and brings light to people's eyes
For she makes me think of Eileen, wherever she may roam, on this side,
    or on that side, of the world

That Dog
by Kathy Kremins

He kept climbing into my lap
that 90-pound dog of amber curls
named after the Irish poet,
plopping himself on my lap,
pinning the book of poems about dogs
by my favorite poet
into my chest as he heaved a sigh.
I must have known then
that his breaths were shortening,
growing quicker,
just as his hair was thinning and whitening.
Three years on, I drive with the baby,
named after the folk singer, in the car seat
checking periodically
(because beauty is fleeting)
on his round red cheeks and radiant smile,
a place to rest my hope.
I catch a glimpse
of that big doodle head bouncing,
tongue out, lips curled in a grin,
gazing at the magical world.
There is pleasure in that moment
when Arlo the child meets
Seamus the dog in that back seat,
cruising down the curvy road
lined with budding magnolias
and early forsythia blooms
with me reciting Mary:
"Listen, whatever you see and love

that's where you are."
It's good to be right here
with no absence present,
surrounded by tendernesses
for a child, a dog, poets, musicians,
and you, wherever you are.

Grave Tending
by Susan Marsh

Burying a crossbill in the garden
I paused to think of where to dig the hole
Where earlier souls didn't sleep already—
Our twenty-year-old cats and ten-year-old catfish,
The nestling warblers from last summer,
And others I did not mean to forget.

I found a place in the raspberry patch
Pale knobby shoots already seeking sky
The soil supple from years of fond attention
Now shrugging off the grip of months in ice.
My spade sank like a talon into the moist soil.

Each spring I grave-tend, planting snow peas
Over the cats and tropical fish and songbirds,
Raking leaves from the knuckles of the iris
And purple fists of columbine over the old dog,
Ground made holy by the ones who lie below.

One night, only a week dead,
His front paws stretched across my chest
I lay awake, not dreaming in the bed
We moved downstairs his last few months
When he could barely hobble to his nest.

I clip the irises, rake the slick wet leaves
Feel once more the soft heft of his paws,
Recall his obstinate male-dog ways,
The hair between his pads gone white
Well before his fifteenth year,
And I hope the flowers will bloom well

More beautiful than ever for him, because of him
I hope the peas grow long and fat over the cats
The berries plump over the newly buried crossbill
And I wonder how I could ever know
Which among them I love best.

War Dog Memorial
Barrington, New Hampshire
by Rodger Martin

Next to the Veterans' Stone sits
an acrylic German Shepherd, panting
for command. In front, a small flag,
a whittled stick, and two large feathers
tied with leather which lift in the breeze.
Like an illusion, the evening summer
haze simmers about a drooping sun.
A distant lawn mower whines like a gnat.

Draped about the Shepherd's neck, dogtags:
Colonel, Roxy, Satan, Cochise. How easy
they trained—anxious, eager—man and dog,
while others strutted the suited wire of duty
and looked down, knowing the dogs
would sense too late, in that sudden crash
of automatic weapons, recognize
like their men all had been forsaken.

The wind turned on my cheek. I saw
Old Barley lift himself at each
late-night mission, wait by the door
acknowledgment and after plod to his bed,
circle three times, and drop, one great sigh
escaping as he drifted into sleep.

Biographies, Acknowledgements of Prior Publication, and Other Books by the Poets in this Volume

Author Biographies

Janet E. Aalfs, founder/director of Lotus Peace Arts at Heron's Bridge/ Valley Women's Martial Arts, former poet laureate of Northampton, MA, 8th degree black belt and Tai Chi instructor, is the author of 3 full-length poetry collections, most recently *What the Dead Want Me to Know*, and several chapbooks. Janet performs weavings of spoken word and martial arts based dance that she calls Poemotion©.

Luther Allen writes poems from his mostly unmanaged 10 acres of mountainside near Bellingham, Washington. His academic work centered mostly on biology and geography; he is a retired building designer. He co-facilitates the SpeakEasy reading series, and was co-editor of *Noisy Water: Poetry from Whatcom County*, Washington (2015). His work is included in numerous journals and anthologies. He views writing as his spiritual practice.

Zeina Azzam, Poet Laureate of the City of Alexandria, Virginia (2022-25), is a Palestinian American poet, writer, editor, and community activist. Publications include *Some Things Never Leave You* (Tiger Bark Press), and *Bayna Bayna, In-Between* (The Poetry Box). She has been nominated twice for a Pushcart Prize, and her poetry is in numerous journals and anthologies. She volunteers for multiple projects including *We Are Not Numbers* and *Grassroots Alexandria*. She earned an M.A. in Arabic literature, an M.A. in sociology, and a B.A. in psychology.

Subhaga Crystal Bacon (they/them), is the author of four collections of poetry including the Lambda Literary Award finalist, *Transitory,* 2023, BOA Editions, Ltd.; and Surrender of Water in Hidden Places, winner of the Red Flag Poetry Chapbook Prize, 2023; A Pushcart and Best of the Net nominee, Subhaga is a teaching artist working in schools and libraries with youth and adults, as well as private students.

H. Byron Ballard, BA, MFA, is a native of Western NC. She is a writer, amateur folklorist with a specialty in Appalachian folk magic & healing. She tours extensively in the US & Great Britain. Her books include four on mountain folk magic. The first was *Staubs and Ditchwater,* and the most recent (2023) is *Small Magics.* She lives in Asheville.

KB Ballentine's latest collection will be forthcoming in Autumn 2024. Current books can be found with Blue Light Press, Iris Press, Middle Creek Publishing, and Celtic Cat Publishing. KB is published in *North Dakota Quarterly, Atlanta Review and Haight-Ashbury Literary Journal,* and others, her work also appears in anthologies including *Women Speak* (2023) and *The Strategic Poet* (2021). www.kbballentine.com

Anne Bergeron's essays and poems appear in *The Hopper, Flyway: A Journal of Writing & Environment, The Dark Mountain Project, Blueline Magazine,* and *Dark Matter: Women Witnessing,* where she is a contributing writer. She is a poet with *Writing the Land: Northeast*, is the 2023 finalist for the Barry Lopez Creative Non-Fiction award at *Cutthroat Journal of the Arts*, and has been twice nominated for a Pushcart Prize. She lives on a homestead in Vermont.

Katherine Hagopian Berry (she/her) is the author of *Mast Year,* (Littoral Books 2020), *LandTrust* (NatureCulture, 2022) and *Orbit*, just released from Toad Hall Editions. Katherine's poems have appeared in many literary magazines, the *Portland Press Herald*, on *Maine NPR* and in multiple anthologies including in the *Writing the Land* series and was a poetry reader for the *Maine Review.*

Jeevan Bhagwat is an award winning poet whose work has been widely published in renowned literary journals across Canada, the U.S. and internationally. His poetry has been anthologized by *Scarborough Arts, The Ontario Poetry Society, the Canadian Authors Association,* and appears in the *National Poetry Registry of Canada.* Jeevan's poetry books include *Luminescence* (IN Publications, 2020) and *The Weight of Dreams* (IN Publications).

Mary Brancaccio is the author of *Fierce Geometry: Poems* (Get Fresh Books, 2022). Her work has appeared in *Terrain.org, Naugatuck River Review, Minerva Rising,* and *Rattle.* She's been a featured poet on *The Slowdown* and the *Poetry Superhighway*. www.ghostgirlpoet.com

Elizabeth M. Burton-Crow, PhD has always felt most at home in wild landscapes and connecting across species. Her doctoral dissertation focused upon the influence of captivity upon the psyches of parrots and poultry. Today, Elizabeth's work strives to integrate ethics, art, and science through her independently run media production and consulting company, the Nature Imaginarium. She is rooted in the Pacific Northwest, with extended animal family.

After she earned two degrees in geology, **Pamela Hobart Carter** became a teacher. Her plays have been produced in Seattle (her home), Montreal (her childhood home), and Fort Worth. Carter is also a visual artist.

Fidelis Fumbui Chiaboh is a Cameroonian poet, playwright, novelist, and critic. His research interest includes investigating the dynamics of cultural pluralism and how diverse cultures are portrayed in contemporary literatures. His published creative works include plays – *Who Got Bih Pregnant* (2019), *Neglected Generation* (2021), a novel – *Buried Before Death* (2021), and a poetry collection *Failed Loves and Lost Lives* (2024)

Dan Close is a poet and novelist living in South Burlington, Vermont. He authored *What the Abenaki Say About Dogs*, poetry which chronicles the lives of the Abenaki of the Champlain basin. His latest poetry collection is entitled *The Night the Moon Went Sailing.* He is a member of the Poetry Society of Vermont and Burlington Writers Workshops. He is a former board member of the League of Vermont Writers. His free time is taken up with wondering what the hell is going to happen next, a pursuit shared by many of his fellow octogenarians.

Candace R. Curran, Buckland, MA, was raised alongside Wachusett Mt. in rural Princeton, MA by a coyote and Ford mechanic doing the best they could. Publications include, *Playing in Wrecks*, Haley's Press, *RAW NerVZ* and *Meat for Tea, the Valley Review.* Curran is the 2022 Elyse Wolf chapbook prize winner, forthcoming from Slate Roof Press.

Patrick Curry, PhD is a Canadian-born writer and scholar who lives in London. He has been a Lecturer at two British universities. He is the author of *Enchantment: Wonder in Modern Life* (2019) and *Art and Enchantment: How Wonder Works* (2023). He is Editor-in Chief of *The Ecological Citizen* (www.ecologicalcitizen.net). More information, including about his poems, can be found on www.patrickcurry.co.uk

Curt G. Curtin was a lifelong poet with six full-length collections, including two for children/young adults. His poems have been published in many anthologies and journals and he's twice been nominated for a Pushcart prize. Awards include: 2010 Frank O'Hara Poetry Award, second place in the 2019 Connecticut Poetry Society contest, and two Arts Council grants to support his work. Curt taught college English and creative writing for 20 years at Westfield State College, MA. He died August 2024. www.curtcurtinpoet.com

Carolyn A. Cushing is a lyric poet inspired by nature, observing our changing climate, and focused on where life and death meet. She also facilitates Soul Path Sanctuary through which she offers inspiration for tending a loving flow between the living and the dead, Tarot sessions, and virtual programs to attune to seasonal wisdom and lunar cycles. A recipient of grants from the Easthampton and Massachusetts Cultural Councils, Carolyn serves as the Poet Laureate of Easthampton, 2023 - 2025. www.soulpathsanctuary.com

Amelia Díaz Ettinger is a BIPOC Mexican/Puerto Rican poet and writer. Her work is highly influenced by Latin American writers including Octavio Paz who describes death as one of Mexican's greatest loves. Her work is a mixture of science, nature, and her struggle for identity and home. She has three full collections of poetry and two chapbooks, another collection of poetry is pending publication for 2025.

Poet **Charlotte Eulette**, lives in Baja California, Mexico and is the director of the Baja Sur Poets and Writers League. The league creates performances showcasing writers including musicians, artists and dancers. She is a co-founder of the Celebrant Foundation & Institute, an organization that teaches the art of ceremony and ritual as a certified Life-Cycle Celebrant. Her books: *Real Vibrant, poems for all that matters, Soul Places, poems that take you there,* and *Life Cycle Ceremonies, A Handbook For Your Whole Life* are available on Amazon.

Victoria Field is a writer and poetry therapist based in Canterbury, Kent, UK. Her creative work includes poetry, drama, fiction, memoir and literary translation. She has co-edited books and published academic papers on therapeutic writing. Her doctoral thesis at Canterbury Christ Church University explored narratives of transformation in pilgrimage. She collaborates with her husband, Eduard Heyning on poetry and music performances, and with geologist, Helen Nattrass on geopoetry.

Wallace Fong's poems have appeared in online publications such as *All Poetry, The Dewdrop, Haiku Universe,* and *Rising Phoenix Review.* He writes a range of poems, from traditional haiku and micro poems to longer free verse poems on themes that center around the beauty and fragility of everything, the joy and travail of being human and the art of mindful living. He retired after many happy years as an academic and currently lives in Singapore with his wife and roomfuls of art.

D. Dina Friedman is the author of two books of poetry: *Here in Sanctuary, Whirling* (Querencia Press) and *Wolf in the Suitcase* (Finishing Line Press); one short-story collection: *Immigrants* (Creators Press) and two young adult novels, *Escaping Into the Night* (Simon and Schuster) and *Playing Dad's Song* (Farrar Straus Giroux). She has published widely literary journals and received four Pushcart Prize nominations for poetry and fiction.

Geri Gale (she/her) is a multi-hyphenate artist (poet, novelist, memoirist, illustrator, narratress). She is a 2024 Jack McCarthy Poetry Book, finalist; 2024 Sally Albiso Poetry Book, honorable mention; 2023 Jack Straw Writer Fellow; and performed in the Moth Seattle Grand Slam. Her award-winning books include *In the Closet: A Triad* (American Fiction Award, LGBTQ+ Fiction Finalist); *Patrice: a poemella* (Silver IPPY: LGBTQ+ Fiction, Independent Publisher Book); and *Waiting: prosepoems* (Dancing Girl Press).

Georgia Gojmerac-Leiner is a poet, board-certified hospital chaplain and a practicing spiritual director. Her recent publications are: poem "Psalm V" in a chapbook anthology *Inside the Seer/Outside the Seen*; Bethany House of Prayer, Arlington, MA, 2018. "The River Kupa;" *Passager,* Winter 2021. "The Supernatural;" *Migrations and Home: The Elements of Place*, 2023. Dr. Gojmerac-Leiner loves to sing. A lover of nature she is an avid walker. She is also a gardener and the family's chef.

Betsy Guttmacher is a Reiki practitioner based in Brooklyn, NY USA who works privately with individuals, and in community and medical settings. Her creative and healing work centers relationships - to ourselves, each other and our planet. She is a member of the Sweet Action poetry collective and a contributor to three of its chapbooks. Her poems can also be found in the *Bullshit Lit 2024 Anthology, Bowery Gothic,* the *Brooklyn Poets Anthology,* and the *Bridge.*

Sharon A. Harmon is a freelance writer and poet. Her chapbooks include *Swimming with Cats* (Autumn Light Press) 2008 and *Wishbone in a Lightning Jar* (Southern Arizona Press) 2017. She is working on a third chapbook, *Trailer Park Children* for early 2025. Sharon can be found on Facebook Sharon A. Harmon Writer & Poet.

James Harpur has published eight books of poetry, including *The Magic Theatre* (2025), a verse memoir of his time at Cambridge University in the late 1970s. His debut novel, *The Pathless Country,* inspired by the teachings of J Krishnnamurti, was winner of the JG Farrell Award and shortlisted for the John McGahern Prize. www.jamesharpur.com

Amy Suzanne Heneveld is a medievalist, writer and teacher living in Vermont. She learned French as a small child living in Geneva, Switzerland, where she later got her PhD in Medieval French Literature from the University of Geneva. When she isn't teaching French, she spends her time translating for the flowers. Her work has been published by Dark Mountain Press and online through her blog at www.enosburghessences.com/cosmic-connection

An 'occasional' poet, much of **Diana Hirst**'s early work was inspired by the landscape of East Kent, particularly its chalklands and its coastline, and she has continued to write about place and its genius loci. She was Deal and Dover Poet of the Year 2008 and has won awards or been listed in the Suffolk, Wivenhoe and Canterbury competitions.

Joan Hofmann is Professor Emerita at the University of Saint Joseph (CT), serves on the Executive Board of Riverwood Poetry, and was the inaugural Poet Laureate of Canton, CT (2015-2019). Her poems are published or forthcoming in various anthologies and journals, including *Writing the Land: The Connecticut River, Waking Up to the Earth, Forgotten Women, Concho River Review, The Tiger Moth Review, Buddhist Poetry Review, Dillydoun Review, Broad River Review,* and *Rumble Fish.* Awards include: Stone Gathering Award and Poetry Society of Michigan Award.

Linea Jantz has worked in a wide range of roles over the years including teaching Business English in Ukraine (pre-invasion), working as a bike law paralegal, and helping film a documentary about women entrepreneurs in the state of Chiapas, Mexico. Her writing features in publications including *Beaver Magazine, EcoTheo Review,* and *Palette Poetry.* She is a past presenter of the *Poetry Moment* for Spokane Public Radio and is the current Writing the Land Poet for the Sunnyside-Snake River Wildlife Area.

Aby Kaupang authored *Radiant Tether, & there's you still thrill hour of the world to love, NOS, disorder not otherwise specified,* and other collections. She holds master's degrees in creative writing and occupational therapy. Working outside of academia, she practices as an occupational therapist and nurse's aide specializing in the treatment of neurodivergent and special needs children. Aby lives in Fort Collins, CO where she assists in organizing an annual book festival, hosts the reading series, EveryEye, and has served as Poet Laureate. abykaupang.com

Kathy Kremins is a retired public school teacher with a BA from the College of St. Elizabeth, an MFA from Goddard College, and a D. Litt. from Drew University. She has two chapbooks of poems, *Seamus & His Smalls* (Two Key Customs, 2023) and *Undressing the World* (Finishing Line Press, 2022). Her full-length poetry collection is *The Curve of Things* (Cavankerry Press, 2024). She is an editor for *NJ Audubon Magazine.*

Sigrun Susan Lane's chapbook, *Salt* (2020) won the Josephine Miles award for excellence in poetry. Her poems appear in regional, national and international publications including the *Amsterdam Quarterly, Ashville Poetry Review, Crab Creek Review, Ekphrastic Review, Seattle Review, Sing Heavenly Muse, Rain City Review, Malahat Review* and others. Awards include those from Seattle and King County Arts Commissions. Lane has published two chapbooks, *Little Bones* and *Salt* (Goldfish Press). She is a docent at the Frye Art Museum in Seattle, WA.

A founder of the Richmond, VA community River City Poets, **Joanna Lee** earned her MD from the Medical College of Virginia and a Master's in neuroscience from William & Mary. Her work has been published in *JAMA, Rattle, Fourth River* and elsewhere and has been nominated for both Pushcart and Best of the Net prizes. She authored *Dissections* (2017) and is a co-editor of *Lingering in the Margins* (2019); she collaborated with the Richmond Symphony to create "Letter to the City." She is the current Poet Laureate for Richmond.

Adria Libolt lives in Bellingham, WA, worked in prisons as a deputy warden and later, taught in a community college. She authored *A Deputy Warden's Reflections on Prison Work* (Wipf & Stock, 2012), and *Food: An Appetite for Life* (White Bird Publications, 2019). She writes essays and poems and has published poems in *Creative Colloquy, Poetry Pigeon, Blue Heron,* among others and anthologies.

Earl Livings is an award-winning poet and fiction writer widely published in Australia and overseas. His writing focuses on science, history, nature, mythology and the sacred. He has published two poetry collections and a fantasy verse novel. Earl lives in Melbourne with his wife and their groaning bookshelves.

Janet MacFadyen's third full-length collection, *State of Grass,* was released February 2024 by Salmon Poetry. Honors include a Massachusetts Cultural Council grant, a 7-month Fine Arts Work Center fellowship in Provincetown, and a Cill Rialaig residency in Ireland. Recent work appears in *Persimmon Tree, White Stag, The High Window, Scientific American, Wordpeace,* several *Writing the Land* anthologies, and *CALYX*. She is Managing Editor of Slate Roof Press, a poetry chapbook collaborative. www.facebook.com/janet.macfadyen

Susan Marsh lives in Jackson, Wyoming. Her poems have appeared in *Deep Wild Journal, Clerestory, Manzanita Review, Parks and Points, Dark Matter, Silver Birch* and other journals and anthologies. Her books include an award-winning novel, *War Creek,* ten non-fiction books, and two poetry chapbooks. She writes a column "Back to Nature" for *Mountain Journal*. www.slmarsh.com

Rodger Martin's *For All The Tea in Zhōngguó,* 2019, follows *The Battlefield Guide,* and The Blue Moon Series selected by Small Press Review as a bi-monthly picks of the year. Awards include: Appalachia award for poetry, NHSCA's award for fiction, and The Stanley Kunitz Medal (2024). His work has been translated and published in China. He's a recipient of numerous fellowships. He was Managing Editor of *The Worcester Review* for 27 years. His latest manuscript, *The Sleeping Dogs of Lubec,* was short-listed for the 2024 Granite State Poetry Prize.

Caitlín Matthews is the author of *Lost Book of the Grail, Celtic Devotional,* and *Celtic Book of the Dead*. Her poetry was published in *Poetry London* by the late Tambimuttu, and many other places. She is known internationally for her work on the mythic and ancestral traditions of Britain and Ireland. www.hallowquest.org.uk

John Matthews is an independent scholar living in Oxford. He has published over 100 titles on Myth, Folklore, and ancient traditions including *The Winter Solstice* (Quest Books, 1999), winner of the Benjamin Franklin Award. He has worked in Film as an historical advisor and won a BAFTA for the movie *King Arthur* (2004). He has made a lifetime study of Arthurian legends, has been a visiting editor for *Arthuriana*, and has contributed to a variety of journals, including *Parabola, The Temenos Academy Review* and *Agenda.*

Felicia Mitchell retired from an award-winning teaching career at Emory & Henry College in 2020 and continues to make her home in the mountains of Virginia, where she enjoys volunteering with the Mt. Rogers Appalachian Trail Club. Poetry publications include *A Mother Speaks, A Daughter Listens: Journeying Together Through Dementia* (Wising Up Press) and *Waltzing with Horses* (Press 53).

Jefferson Navicky is the author of four books, most recently *Head of Island Beautification for the Rural Outlands* (2023) as well as *Antique Densities: Modern Parables & Other Experiments on Short Prose* (2021), which won the 2022 Maine Literary Award for Poetry. He works as the archivist for the Maine Women Writers Collection and lives in rural midcoast Maine.

Heather Pankl (they/them) grew up in New Jersey to an east Tennessee family, lived in Oregon for 10 years, and has called Maryland home since 2000. Publication credits include *Oregon East Magazine,* indie zines *Sola* and *Dog Poetry, Rain Magazine* (Clatsop Community College), *Poets Reading the News,* and *Poems from the Wellspring* (as Heather Livingston). Their poem, "Window," was chosen for inclusion in Oregon East's 50th anniversary edition.

Charles A. Perrone was born in the Empire State of New York, grew up in the Golden State of California, last studied in the Lone Star State of Texas, finished his working days in the Sunshine State of Florida, and returned to the West Coast to enjoy retirement between the seashore and the redwoods. His not-so-secret-anymore life as a published poet spans the Americas and the oceans, as well as the Internet. The poetry has appeared in books and journals (print and digital) in USA, Canada, UK, Mexico, Brazil, and Australia.

Robert Eugene Perry is a native of Massachusetts and author of five books, the latest *Earthsongs* (Human Error Publishing, 2022). His poetry has appeared in numerous anthologies & publications. He was a finalist in the 2023 Beals Prize for Poetry and his poem Heard Steet/ Hadwen Park in Winter was a winner in WCPA's 2024 Poems in and out of Places. Perry has emceed the monthly Open Mic at Booklovers' Gourmet in Webster, MA since 2017.
www.roberteugeneperry.myportfolio.com

Katherine Pierpoint was born in the UK, and lives in Canterbury, sometimes Glastonbury. She is a writer, a qualified energy-healer (College of Psychic Studies, London, 2022), and a literary translator for the Poetry Translation Centre, London. Her collection of poems, *Truffle Beds,* was shortlisted for a T.S.Eliot prize, and received the Society of Authors' Somerset Maugham Award.

k pihl resides in Connecticut, and has recently published her first book, *omphaloskepsis*, (Alien Buddha Press, 2024). pihl's poetry is often confessional, examining the experiences that shape us, and asking, in the great tradition of Michael Scott, why are we the way that we are? pihl was the 2011 Dorothy

McCollum Siebert Award winner at Eastern University and has been performing her poetry (sporadically) ever since.

Suzanne S. Rancourt, Abenaki/Huron, Quebecois, Scottish descent, USMC and Army Veteran. Awards include: NU Press & Native Writers' Circle of the Americas and Poetry of Modern Conflict. Author of *Billboard in the Clouds*, *murmurs at the gate*, *Old Stones, New Roads*, and *Songs of Archilochus*. Suzanne is a multimodal EXAT, CASAC, w/ degrees in psych., writing, Aikido, Iaido; a Writing the Land Fellow; Guest Artist at UMI's New England Literature Program, Sundog Poetry Center, and Solstice MFA. www.expressive-arts.com

Elaine Reardon's first chapbook, *The Heart is a Nursery For Hope*, won first honors from Flutter Press in 2016. Her second chapbook, *Look Behind You*, was also published by Flutter Press. Most recently Elaine's work was published in *The Common, Galway Review, Pensive Journal,* and similar journals. A new chapbook, *Stories Told In A Forgotten Tongue* will be published by Finishing Line Press in September 2024. www.elainereardon.wordpress.com

Kate Rex: A bio in 70 words! Not quite enough for one word for each year of my life. What matters distilled, put into some kind of pattern, here goes…..I live on the edge of groups. constantly watchful, professionally snarky holding onto who and what matters, throwing out the rest. I work with words and images in the South of France, Glasgow Scotland and in the spaces between. Three words left….

Laura Rodley's latest books are *Turn Left at Normal* by Big Table Press, *Counter Point* by Prolific Press, and *Ribbons and Moths Poems for Children* by Kelsay Books that won Children's Non-fiction in the International Book Awards. She is a Pushcart Prize winner.

رمزي سالم
شاعر فلسطيني، ولد في ٦ مارس ١٩٩٦ في غزة ويقيم حالياً في بلجيكا، نشر العديد من القصائد بلغات متعددة. يعتزم إصدار أول مجموعة شعرية له هذا العام، والتي تستكشف مواضيع الفقدان والمعاناة وتآكل الإنسانية. تعكس أعماله تجاربه من القلق والخوف والشوق والحنين إلى الوطن كوافد، بالإضافة إلى الحرب والمأساة في غزة.

Amanda (Giles) Shedonist is a free-spirited poet from NH. She hosts the poetry share at SpiritFire festival and edited an accompanying anthology. She believes strongly in the magic you contain and will go to great lengths to tease it out if you let her. Her poems have published in the anthologies Soul Expressions *Poetry Anthology: Volume 1* (independently published) and *Lunation* from the Portsmouth Poet Laureate Program and Senile Monk Press (NH) as well as in her own chapbook *I have questions…*

Yehudit Silverman, M.A. R-DMT, RDT Former Chair, Department of Creative Arts Therapies, Concordia University, Montreal, is the published author of several articles, OpEds, poetry, and book, *The Story Within – myth and fairy tale in therapy*. An award - winning documentary filmmaker on issues around suicide and interfaith dialogue, she presents internationally and was featured on *PBS television, Global News, Authority Magazine,* and *La Presse.* www.yehuditsilverman.com

M. Anne Sweet is a poet and artist who has performed and exhibited throughout the Pacific Northwest. She has performed individually, as well as with The Seattle Five Plus One, Project Z, and Daughters of Dementia. Credits include a poetry collection, *Nailed to the Sky*; three graphic poem chapbooks; and numerous works in publication. She maintains a working studio in Seattle, where her visual art pieces frequently combine her art and poetry.

Steve Trombulak is a pagaian who works to heal the connections between community and the more-than-just-human world. His poetry draws from his almost 40 years as an academic biologist specializing in conservation biology and natural history. His most recent work is *The Way of Gaia*, with Martin Bridge, a visual and textual exploration of the past, present, and future of the Tree of Life (NatureCulture, 2022).

Tommy Twilite (aka Thomas Richard Clark) has published numerous chapbooks, *Fifty Words for Rain* (Florence Poets Society Press, 2021), and several albums of original music. Awards include: National Beat Poetry Foundation Massachusetts Beat Poet Laureate (2021-2023) and New Generation Beat Poet Laureate (2024-Lifetime). Tommy is the Co-founder and Director of the Florence Poets Society, and the host of the *Twilite Poetry Pub* on WXOJ-FM. He believes that poetry and music can change the world.

Angela (Angie) Trudell Vasquez, a second and third generation Mexican-American originally from Iowa, served as the city of Madison, Wisconsin Poet Laureate from 2020 to early 2024. She earned her MFA from the Institute of American Indian Arts. Her fourth poetry collection, *My People Redux,* was published in January 2022.

Lisa "Rubi G." Ventura (she/her) is a Washington Heights-bred Black Dominican poet, essayist, performer, teaching artist, and author of *¿Con qué papel me envuelves la luna?* Her work has been published and showcased by numerous literary platforms and arts organizations. She's been a featured poet for Morris-Jumel Mansion and Nuyorican Poets Café. Lisa is a 2024 mentee for the Latinx-in-Publishing program and a VONA 2022 alumni. www.lapoetarubi.com

Linda Warren's poems have appeared in such journals as *The Worcester Review, Diner, Whiskey Island Magazine,* and in *Writing the Land* anthologies. She is a past winner of a Frank O'Hara prize for poetry, and has been nominated for a Pushcart. She has served as an editor of *The Worcester Review,* and on the board of the Worcester County Poetry Association. She fishes the trout and salmon rivers of New England and New Brunswick as often as she can, and has a collection of poems inspired by those rivers forthcoming from Finishing Line Press.

Rhett Watts lives in Central MA with her husband and Siberian cat. A trained spiritual companion, she facilitates writing and SoulCollage® workshops. Her poems have appeared in many journals. Her books are: *Willing Suspension* (Antrim House Books, 2014), *The Braiding* (Kelsay Books, 2019) and coming in 2025, *The Double Nest* (Fernwood Press). Rhett agrees with the late great Maurice Sendak who said, "Everyone should be quiet near a little stream and listen."

Joe Webster lives and writes in Boston, MA, his hometown, on Massachusett people's land. Themes and images of nature, family, and beauty appear in his work. He reads at open mics and at poetry groups across the city and is active in environmental justice work there. He has been published in the Trident Poetry Collective chapbook *The Heartbreaks*, Boston, Amazon KDP, 2024.

Dorinda Wegener's first full-length collection is *Four Fields*, (Trio House Press, 2024). She is a *Poets & Writers Magazine* 2024 Get The Word Out Poetry Cohort Participant. Wegener is a poet and an essayist with work in *LitHub, THRUSH, Mid-American Review, Indiana Review, Ethel, Hayden's Ferry Review* and *Hunger Mountain.* She is a Perianesthesia Certified Registered Nurse in Richmond, VA, who holds an MFA in Poetry from New England College, where she was a Joel Oppenheimer Award Recipient. www.dorindawegener.com

Heidegger's biography of Aristotle, which he thought should be a template for all artists and writers, reads: "He was born, he thought, he died. All the rest is pure anecdote." **Roger West** would like you to know he is not dead yet. Living proof can be found on You Tube - rogerwestmusic - and on Facebook - Strangers Among Their People.

Meg Weston is a poet, non-fiction writer, and photographer with passion for the geological processes that shape the earth and the stories that shape our lives. As co-founder of ThePoetsCorner.org and the Camden Festival of Poetry, and board member of Millay House Rockland, Meg supports the poetry community. Her poems have appeared in journals and anthologies. Publications include a poetry collection, *Magma Intrusions* (2023) and two chapbooks: *Letters from the White Queen* (2020), and *To the Point and Back: Swimming Poems* (2024). www.volcanoes.com

Judith Yarnall is a writer and retired teacher of humanities who lives by Lake Champlain in Vermont. She published *Transformations of Circe,* a cultural history of that Homeric character (University of Illinois Press). Her poems and essays have appeared in various journals, most recently *The Medical Literary Messenger.* She thanks her Montreal-based writers' group, who were the first audience for "The Third Night" appearing here. It was written right after the death of her middle daughter, the painter Kate True, in November 2023.

About the Editor

Deirdre Pulgram-Arthen has a passion for creating deeply spiritual, personal experiences of the sacred—in recognition of ourselves as a part of the natural world, and as a way of expanding our connections within the human community. As the director of EarthSpirit, a non-profit focused on current and traditional European earth-centered spiritualities, she creates rituals for celebration, seasonal cycles and rites of passage—including the sacred passage into death. By using music and poetry to reach beyond rational thought and touch the depths of our felt experience, the arts serve as passageways for transformation and healing. Deirdre has worked in service to her local, spiritual, and interfaith communities for 40 years. She has a graduate degree in counseling psychology, is a certified Death Midwife, and a published author and composer of sacred chants. She is a mother and a grandmother, which is her favorite title. Deirdre lives in the Berkshire hills of western Massachusetts with a small community on a 130 acre nature preserve. www.earthspirit.com

About the Foreword Author

Born and brought up in Liverpool, as an adult I have moved 25 miles away to Chester. I have trained and worked as a teacher, a social worker, and up to the present day as a psychotherapist. I am a wife and a mother to three children and a grandmother of four. My late son Jon started Death Cafe and we worked on this project together; since his death my daughter Jools and Irun it. My leisure time is spent seeing family and friends, I have recently restarted piano lesssons and sing in two choirs. www.deathcafe.com

About the Publisher

Lis McLoughlin, PhD is the founder and director of NatureCulture LLC. She has degrees in Civil Engineering, Education, and Science and Technology Studies. She lives off-grid in Northfield, Massachusetts and part-time in Montréal, Québec. Her mission is to help people be in right relationship with the rest of Nature. www.nature-culture.net www.writingtheland.org

About the Artist

Martin Bridge carries his family tradition forth as he lives, creates, and teaches in Western Massachusetts. His work spans a wide range of media: Drawing, Painting, Sculpture, Theater Design, Site Specific Installations, and Performance. As an avid Permaculture designer he strives to improve his awareness of how he relates to the natural world and to live in better balance. Through his work he hopes to inspire and cultivate a greater sense of mystery and possibility.
www.thebridgebrothers.com

Acknowledgements of Prior Publication

Allen, Luther. "merge" was first published in *Vanishing into the Leaves, Poems from Ocean Wilderness*, edited by Patrick Lane. Lantzville, BC, Canada: Leaf Press. 2014.

Azzam, Zeina:
"Comet" was previously published in *Plume,* June 2023.
"Death Arrives" and "You Could Tell Yourself" were previously published in *Some Things Never Leave You.* Rochester, NY: Tiger Bark Press. 2023.

Bergeron, Anne. An earlier version of "Losing the Child, Haad Tien, Thailand," can be found in *Flyway: Journal of Writing and Environment*, Fall/Winter 2020.

Bhagwat, Jeevan. "How the Living Carry The Dead" previously published in Bhagwat, Jeevan. *Luminescence*. Waban, MA: IN Publications. 2020.

Carter, Pamela Hobart. "Succession" previously published in *Burningword 96, Burningword Literary Journal,* October 2020.

Close, Dan. All poems from Close, Dan. *The Night the Moon Went Sailing.* Burlington, VT: Onion River Press. 2023.

Curran, Candace R.:
"Blues Hound" previously appeared in *Poems Around Town; In the Time of Covid.* Brattleboro, VT: Small Pond Press. 2021.
"Mausoleum" and "How Does One Survive" previously appeared in a similar form in *Bone Cages, poems by Candace R. Curran and others.* Athol, MA: Haley's.1996.
"In the Dark" was taken from the poem "In the Dark" Curran, Candace. *The Sound of Her Good Name.* Northfield, MA: Slate Roof Press. Forthcoming 2025.

Cushing, Carolyn A. "First Anniversary Prayers" was first published on *Writing in a Woman's Voice,* May 2020.

Eulette, Charlotte:
"When Friends Die," "Circle of Tears," "Tranquilo" are from *Real. Vibrant, poems for all that matters.* Self-published on Amazon, October 2020.
"November 30th, 11:45PM Central Time" is from *Soul Places, poems that take you there.* Self-published on Amazon, June 2024.

Victoria Field:
"Forget-Me-Nots" and "Tides" first appeared in *Olga's Dreams*. 2004.
"Father" first appeared in *Many Waters.* 2006
"Opening the Gate" first appeared in *The Lost Boys*. 2013.
All from Canterbury, UK: fal publications.

Friedman, D. Dina: "What I Might Say to Death" was originally published in *Gordon Square Review*, November 2020.

Harmon, Sharon A.:
"Poetic Madness" was previously published in *Worcester Magazine*. 2015.
"The Grief Mobile" was previously published in *Swimming with Cats*. Warwick, MA: Autumn Light Press. 2008.

Harpur, James. "The Frame of Furnace Light" was first published in *The Monk's Dream*. Vancouver, BC: Anvil Press. 1995.

Hofmann, Joan. "Keepers," was originally published in slightly different version in *Shapes, Literary Journal of Manchester Community College*, CT, 2014.

Kremins, Kathy. "That First Walk" and "That Dog" first published in Kremins, Kathy. *Seamus & His Smalls*. Delaware: Two Key Customs Press. 2023.

Livings, Earl:
"Black, with One White Spot" was previously published in Livings, Earl. *Libation*. Port Adelaide, South Australia: Ginninderra Press. 2018.
"Bees Dance" was previously published in *Australian Poetry Anthology, Volume 9 (2021-2022)*. Australian Poetry Ltd, Naarm, Melbourne. 2021.

MacFadyen, Janet:
"The Future Melts" first appeared in the *Daily Hampshire Gazette*, and later appeared in the *Provincelands*. Northfield, MA: Slate Roof Press. 2012.
"In Defense of Stones" first appeared in *Sanctuary*, The Journal of the Massachusetts Audubon Society, Sept/Oct 1994, and later in *In Defense of Stones*. Whately, MA: Heatherstone Press. 1995.

Martin, Rodger:
"Lullaby for my mother" was first published in *Poetry South*, 2010, Yazoo River Press, Ita Bina, MS. p. 21.
"The War Dog Memorial" was first published in *The 2008 Poets' Guide to NH*, PSNH. 2007. p. 11.

Mitchell, Felicia:
"For a Survivor Who Sits With Death" previously published in *Hospital Drive: The Literature and Humanities Journal of the UVA School of Medicine*, under the title "For Eliza, Who Sits With Death"
"Revelation at Philpot Lake" previously published in Mitchell, Felicia. *Waltzing with Horses*. Winston-Salem, NC: Press 53. 2014.

Navicky, Jefferson:
"Moon Review at the Emergency Vet" originally appeared in *Southern Humanities Review*, Volume 56, No. 2, Summer 2023.
"My Father Could Take Apart a Dryer" originally appeared in *Beloit Poetry Journal,* Volume 70, No. 1, Spring 2020.

Perrone, Charles A. "A Memo to the Curious" previously appeared in the e-book *A Cross-Country Change of Plans.* Newhall, CA: Poetry Super Highway. 2023.

Perry, Robert Eugene:
"Everything Belongs," "Orphan," and "October Ghost" first appeared in *Earthsongs.* Wendell, MA: Human Error Press. 2022.

Reardon, Elaine. "What She Saved" was previously published in *Culinary Origami,* an online magazine, 2013.

Rodley, Laura. "Flight Path" was previously published in *The Galway Review* on 10/13/22 as well as *Autumn Sky Daily* on 11/16/22.

رمزي سالم، "أقدام تسبق الفجر"، تم نشرها في العربي في يناير 2024

Shedonist (Giles), Amanda. "Let her eat cake" previously appeared in *Soul Expressions Poetry Anthology: Volume 1.* Barrington NH: SpiritFire Publishing. 2018. It contains an excerpt of the poem "Thin Woman" by Michelle Neve, previously published in *Within This Circle: Ix'Chel Jaguar's Collected Works Volume II.* Scotts Valley, CA: CreateSpace Independent Publishing. 2014. Reprinted with permission.

Silverman, Yehudit:
"Gutted" and "Lingering" were read on *Writers Radio,* March 27, 2024.

Vasquez, Angela (Angie) Trudell. "Sea Burial" appeared in *In Light, Always Light.* Georgetown, KY: Finishing Line Press. 2019.

Wegener, Dorinda:
"The Fourth Child," "Yield," and "Trappings" have appeared in *Four Fields.* Minneapolis, MN: Trio House Press. 2024. Reprinted with permission of the publisher.

Other Books by the Poets in this Volume

Aalfs, Janet E.:
Reach. Florence, MA: Perugia Press. 1999.
Bird of a Thousand Eyes. Amherst, MA: Levellers Press. 2010.
What the Dead Want Me to Know. Wendell, MA: Human Error Publishing. 2022.
Full Open. Northampton, MA: Orogeny Press. 1996.
Of Angels and Survivors. Amherst, MA: Two Herons Press. 1992.
Lubec Tides. Northampton, MA: Thousand Hands Press. 2007.

Allen, Luther:
The View from Lummi Island, a journal of excursion into place, (2010) and *A Spiritual Thread* (2024), both from Bellingham, WA: Other Mind Press.

Ballentine, KB:
All the Way Through. Los Angeles, CA: Sheila-Na-Gig. Forthcoming 2024.
Spirit of Wild (2023), *The Light Tears Loose* (2019), *Perfume of Leaving* (2016), and *What Comes of Waiting* (2013). San Francisco, CA: Blue Light Press.
Edge of an Echo. Oak Ridge, TN: Iris Press. 2021.
Almost Everything, Almost Nothing. Beulah Valley, CO: Middle Creek Publishing. 2017.
Fragments of Light (2009) and *Gathering Stones* (2008) Knoxville, TN: Celtic Cat Publishing.

Carter, Pamela Hobart:
Her Imaginary Museum. American Fork, UT: Kelsay Books. 2020.
Held Together with Tape and Glue. Georgetown, KY: Finishing Line Press. 2021.
Behind the Scenes at the Eternal Everyday (2023), and *Only Connect* (2024). Bangalore, India: Yavanika Press.

Close, Dan. *The Night the Moon Went Sailing.* Burlington, VT: Onion River Press. 2023.

Curran, Candace R.:
The Sound of Her Good Name. Northfield, MA: Slate Roof Press. Forthcoming 2025.
Playing in Wrecks: Poems New and Used (2011); *Bone cages: poems* (ed et alia) (1996); *Copper Silhouette: poems* (1995); *Harness: nature-based poetry focusing on human and seasonal experience* (1994); and *Bugaboos: situational poetry* (1993). Athol, MA: Haley's.

Curtin, Curt G.:
In Our Name. San Francisco, CA: Atticus Publishing, 2024.
Nature's Eclectic Designs (2023), *So Much Depends on Where You Live* (2022), *Why Trees Sneeze and Other Mysteries* (2021), *Kerry Dancers* (2020), *For Art's Sake* (2019). American Fork, UT: Kelsay Books.

Ettinger, Amelia Díaz:
Speaking at a Time. La Grande, OR: Redbat Press. 2015.
Learning to Love a Western Sky. Portland, OR: Airlie Press. 2020.

Fossils on a Red Flag. Georgetown, KY: Finishing Line Press. 2021.
Self-Dissection. Portland, OR: The Poetry Box. 2023.
Between the Eye of the Lizard and the Moon. Forthcoming from Redbat Press, 2024.
These Hollowed Bones. Barnstable, MA: Sea Crow Press. 2024.

Eulette, Charlotte:
Soul.Places, poems that take you there (2024) and *Real.Vibrant, poems for all that matters* (2020). Self-published on Amazon.

Field, Victoria:
Sturua, L. (2023). *On the Contrary* (N. Bukia-Peters & V. Field, Trans.). Canterbury, England: fal publications.
Field, V. *A Speech of Birds* (2020) and *Baggage: A Book of Leavings* (2016). London, England: Francis Boutle Publishers.

Friedman, D. Dina:
Here in Sanctuary—Whirling. Chicago, IL: Querencia Press. 2024.
Wolf in the Suitcase. Georgetown, KY: Finishing Line Press. 2019.

Harpur, James:
The White Silhouette. Manchester: Carcanet. 2018.
The Magic Theatre (2025) and *The Examined Life* (2021). Reading: Two Rivers Press.
The Oratory of Light. Glasgow: Wild Goose Press. 2021.

Hofmann, Joan:
Coming Back. Bloomfield, CT: Antrim House. 2014.
Alive (2017) and *Alive, Too* (2019). West Hartford, CT: Grayson Press.

Kaupang, Aby:
Radiant Tether. Chicago, IL: Verge Books. 2023.
NOS (DISORDER, NOT OTHERWISE SPECIFIED). New York, NY: Futurepoem Books. 2018.
Little "g" God Grows Tired of Me. Denver, CO: SpringGun Press. 2013.
Absence Is Such a Transparent House. Huntington Beach, CA:Tebot Bach. 2011.
& there's you still thrill hour of the world to love. Anderson, SC: Parlor Press / Free Verse Ed. 2003.

Kremins, Kathy:
The Curve of Things. Fort Lee, NJ: Cavankerry Press. 2024.
Undressing the World. Georgetown, KY: Finishing Line Press. 2022.

Lee, Joanna:
Dissections. Georgetown, KY: Finishing Line Press. 2017.
Lingering in the Margins: A River City Anthology (Co-edited with Judy Melchiorre and Marsha Owens). Richmond, VA: Chop Suey Books. 2019.

Livings, Earl. *Libation.* Port Adelaide, South Australia: Ginninderra Press. 2018.

Marsh, Susan:
This Earth Has Been Too Generous. Georgetown, KY: Finishing Line Press. 2022.
Passings. Chicago, IL: Dancing Girl Press. 2024.

Martin, Rodger:
Selection of New Chinese and American Pastoral Poems. Nanjing, PRC: Yangtze River Journal. 2015.
Paradise Lost adapted for Dramatic Reading: co-editor B. Eugene McCarthy. 12 Booklets with essays. Hancock, NH: Monadnock Pastoral Poets. 2014.
The Blue Moon Series (2006, 2009), *The Battlefield Guide* (2007, 2010) and *For All The Tea in Zhōngguó* (2019). Concord, NH: Hobblebush Books.
On The Monadnock: The New American Pastoral Poets. (Zhang Ziqing, Ed). Beijing, China. 2006.

Matthews, Caítlin:
The Art of Celtic Seership. London: Watkins. 2021.
The Celtic Book of the Dead. Atglen, PA: Schiffer. 2023.
The Celtic Devotional. Queensland, Australia: Animal Dreaming. 2024.
Diary of a Soul Doctor (2016) and *Return of the Soul Doctor* (2020). Traverse City, MI: Star Seed Books.
Walkers Between the Worlds: The Western Mysteries from Shaman to Magus (2004); *King Arthur and the Goddess of the La* (2002); *Mabon and the Guardians of Celtic Britain* (2002); *Lost Book of the Grail* (2019). Rochester, VT: Inner Traditions.
Sophia, Goddess of Wisdom: Bride of God. Newburyport, MA: Quest, 2001.

Matthews, John:
Arthur of Albion. Concord, MA: Barefoot Books. 2008/2018.
The Book of Merlin (2020) and *Artorius: The Real King Arthur* (2020). Stroud, England: Amberley.
Celtic Myths & Legends (with Caítlin Matthews). London: Folio Society. 2006.
Celtic Verse. London, England: Watkins. 2007-2021.
Element Encyclopaedia of Magical Creatures (2005) and *The Great Book of King Arthur & His Knights* (2022). New York: HarperCollins.
The Grail: Quest for the Eternal. London: Thames & Hudson. 1981.
Le Morte D'Arthur: First Annotated Edition. Ann Arbor, MI: Chaosium. 2024.
Mystery of Spring Heeled Jack. Rochester, VT: Inner Traditions. 2017.

Perrone, Charles A.:
Designs: Blueprints of Floorplans of a Provisional Residence. Allahabad, India: cyberwit. 2002.
A CAPacious Act (2017), *Out of Alphabetical Order* (2015), and *six seven* (2008). Chicago, IL: moriapoetry.
halves and have nots. p.o.w. 19 [Series 4]. Edinburgh, Scotland: Unit4art. 2014.
deliranjo. Florianóplis, Brazil: Katarina Kartonera. 2013.

Perry, Robert Eugene:
Earthsongs (2022) and *Surrendering to the Path* (2020). Wendell, MA: Human Error Publishing.
if only i were a mystic this would all come so easy (2011), *The Sacred Dance: Poetry to Nourish the Spirit* (2008), and *Where The Journey Takes You* (2007). Dudley, MA: REP Publishing.

Pierpoint, Katherine. *Truffle Beds.* London, England: Faber & Faber. 1995.

Shedonist (Giles), Amanda:
Soul Expressions Poetry Anthology: Volume 1. Barrington NH: SpiritFire Publishing. 2018.
*I have questions....*Barrington, NH: Self-Published. 2024.

(Bridge, M., and) **Steve Trombulak.***The Way of Gaia.* Northfield, MA: NatureCulture LLC. 2023.

Vasquez, Angela (Angie) Trudell:
My People Redux (2022) and *In Light, Always Light* (2019). Georgetown, KY: Finishing Line Press.

Wegener, Dorinda. *Four Fields.* Minneapolis, MN: Trio House Press, 2024.

Epilogue

The Frame of Furnace Light
by James Harpur

—"Each of us finds the world of death fitted to himself." After Aeneid Book VI:743

1 Visiting

It could be the departure lounge at Athens:
Sound-proof glass, anxious Arabs, Greeks, swept marble.
Only the deep lifts hint at any menace.

Within the silent maze of corridors
My mind winds up as I close in on my goal
Dry-mouthed like Theseus sensing the Minotaur.

Room 303 – there he is! Half man, half bed,
Bellowing with laughter, his blubbery belly
Quivering above the sheets, his twitchy head

Ablaze with pre-op nerves and quickfire jokes,
A bull tycoon as helpless as a puppy
Eager for pats and reassuring strokes.

At length I leave. My unravelled mind is led
From trail to trail, but cannot keep the thread.

2 Intensive Care

A realm of coming back and passing over
It lies below the ground behind sealed doors.
I give the password, cross the threshold, enter

And see moving tableaux from a scene in hell:
Robed psychopomps and flickering monitors
Masked neophytes equipped with charts and needles

A line of slabs adorned with naked creatures
Collapsed like boneless chickens and restrained
By wires, their stomachs laddered black in stitches.

I sit beside my specimen, who lies
With punctured throat and softly sagging head
And hope that when at last he lifts his eyes

He sees the bleared face of his youngest son
Not the impatient bristling brows of Charon.

3 Last Visit

A Friday evening in the year of drought
The open window flicked with flying insects
The room was soft with balmy air and light.

My ailing father plumped in bed seemed carefree
As if a long-term deadline had been met.
Relaxed, we chatted, idly watched TV...

If I had known it was to be our last time
At what moment could I have departed
Ever adding seconds of his life to mine?

As it was I picked a random pause to go,
As usual kissed the scar on his bald head
And with a 'see you soon' stepped out into

The lamplight of the slow embalming summer
Which seemed as if it would last forever.

4 Cremation

The hearse sharks through the shoals of Putney
Homing towards the bloodless drive-in chapel,
Bearing our father on his final journey.

A scattering of family, friends, we try
To sing to life this nuclear funeral.
The unknown vicar speaks...we kneel to pray

And watch the climax of the rite of passage:
The coffin sliding into the furnace
With the panache of airport reclaim baggage.

Outside, as yet more mourners wait, we return
To sanguine selves, taking home the ashes
Of all he was within a plastic urn,

Numbing out the absence, the ritual vacuum,
The last reductio ad absurdum.

5 Naming of Parts

The lungs that sucked the foaming Irish Sea
The tongue that sprung its traps of wit and puns
The nails that plucked the twinkling ukelele

The feet that trod the mud towards the Po
The hands that fed the water-cooled machine guns
The ears that heard the silence at Cassino

The freckled scalp that gashed a stalactite
The arm that kept a tennis rally going
The eyes that saw the comet burn the night

Have duly carried out their mortal service
And free from tyranny of endless doing
Have come to rest in blissfulness of peace

As dead appendages of coffined flesh
The gorgeous flames will turn to fiery ash.

6 Memorial Service

Although the images dim, my mind recalls
A sharpened turquoise morning in September

The sun burning Blackfriars and St Paul's

And people ghosting into church – the cast
Of his life, each a living tessera,
A tiny embered memory of his past

And, unforgettable, Fauré's Requiem,
Abide with Me, Swing Low Sweet Chariot,
The burnished echoes of Jerusalem.

Afterwards, friends and cronies from his club
Flowed out through the frame of furnace light
And brother soldiers slipped off to the pub

To blink at gun-flash memories of the Po
To blank out who would be the next to go.

7 Last Rites

A coastguard pilot in his spotter plane
Took off towards the tight-lipped sky above
Bearing the urn of carbon flesh and bone.

Clouds softened and with a gradual smile the sun
Caressed the humming craft into a dove
Winging its shadow to the flecked horizon.

Unseen the dusty atoms drifted down
Acquiesced on the surface of the sea
Completing the final dissolution.

Now beady darting fish invade his grave
His tombstone is every ship that passes by
Nothing remains but litanies of wave on wave

Rushing over gravelly shores where they release
Their hushed prayers, rest in peace, in peace, in peace...

Index

Poems Suggested for use in Ritual

Poems Organized by Relationship to Deceased

** suggested for use in ritual*

Poems Organized by Theme
** suggested for use in ritual*

Poems in Languages other than English
** suggested for use in ritual*

Reflections, Thoughts, and Notes

Milton Keynes UK
Ingram Content Group UK Ltd.
UKHW050930301024
450117UK00022B/32

9 781960 293114